First Course:
Data Structures and
Algorithms Using Java

First Course:
Data Structures and
Algorithms Using Java

Dr. Edward Hill, Jr.

iUniverse, Inc.
New York Lincoln Shanghai

First Course: Data Structures and Algorithms Using Java

iUniverse, Inc.

For information address:
iUniverse, Inc.
2021 Pine Lake Road, Suite 100
Lincoln, NE 68512
www.iuniverse.com

ISBN: 0-595-31896-7

Printed in the United States of America

Contents

Preface

Use as a Textbook

The design and analysis of efficient data structures has been recognized as a key subject in computing. The study of data structures is part of the core curriculum in computer science and computer engineering. Typically, in programs based upon semesters, elementary data structures are introduced in the first programming course. In some computer science curriculums in the first semester a major high level programming language with laboratory work is studied. This is followed by a second semester programming course in the same programming language that emphasizes many of the advance features in the language. After two semesters of programming in a specific programming language the students are introduced to their first semester course in data structures. This first course in data structures covers introductory topics on linked stacks, linked queues, linked deques, lists, trees, hashing, text processing, file structures, and inverted files. Emphasis is on data structures and their use in programming. Students are encouraged to design and implement data structures and programs in their high level programming language to support their data structures. The idea is to apply data structures and improve the programming skills in the high level programming language. Emphasis is placed on the thinking necessary to think links. To enforce this paradigm a data structure model (DSM) is introduced to emulate a few constructs from the List Processing (LISP) language. Each data structure is defined and developed in a paradigm used in geometry to show the relationships and differences in the data structures. Algorithms are designed to detail the steps to design and implement the data structures. Emphasis is placed on writing methods in Java to enforce strong modular programming style and skills. A second course in Data Structures builds on the introduction and introduces more details and other topics in data structures. All exercises are programming problems to sharpen the programming skills and enhance the knowledge of data structures. These topics are not treated for completeness. For example the Lists chapter implements the fundamentals of list processing and does not cover topics on garbage collection, available storage management, etc.

Prerequisites

This book is written assuming that the reader comes to it with certain knowledge. It is assumed that the reader is familiar with a high level programming language, such as Java or C++. The reader understands the main constructs from such a high level language, including:

- Variables and expressions
- Methods or functions
- Decision structures (such as if-statements, and switch-statements)
- Iteration structures (for-loops and while-loops)
- Class definition and use
- Object definition and use.

For readers who are familiar with these concepts, but not with how they are expressed in Java, a data structure model is used to minimize the knowledge of class and object definitions in Java. A DSM is used to emphasize data structures and use Java to implement designs to enforce a level of knowledge on data structures and enhance programming skill in Java.

For the Instructor

This book is intended primarily as a textbook for a first semester Sophomore Data Structures course in which the students have studied two semesters of the Java programming language. It is assumed that a more advanced second course in Data Structures is studied that emphasizes Priority Queues, Search trees, Sorting, Graphics, and other topics.

1

Introduction

The needs for data structures are vase in the implementation of programs on computers. Data structures organize data and lead to the implementation of more efficient programs. Computers are more powerful and applications are more complex. More complex applications demand more calculations and the use of data structures.

Data organized as a collection of records can be searched, processed in any order, or modified. The choice of data structures and algorithm can make the difference between a program running in a few seconds or many days. Program design and implementation must employ an efficiency paradigm. A solution is said to be efficient if it solves the problem within its resource constraints of space and time. The cost of a solution is the amount of resource units that the solution consumes.

Selecting a Data Structure

Selecting a data structure for a problem is a critical factor in the design and implementation of programs. Analyze the problem to determine the resource constraints a solution must meet. Determine the basic operations that must be supported. Operations that are considered are insertions or deletions at the beginning, interspersed with other operations, or those arriving and leaving according to some statistical distribution. Quantify the resource constraints for each operation. Select the data structure that best meets these requirements.

Data Structure Philosophy

Each data structure has costs and benefits. Rarely is one data structure better than another in all situations. A data structure requires space for each data item it stores, time to perform each basic operation, and a programming effort. Each problem has constraints on available space and time. Only after a careful analysis of problem characteristics can we know the best data structure for the task.

Goals of This Text

Reinforce the concept that costs and benefits that exist for data structures. Apply the commonly used data structures. Measure the cost of a data structure or program. These techniques also allow you to judge the merits of new data structures that you or others might invent.

1.1. Definition of Data Structure

Abstract Data Type

An Abstract Data Type (ADT) is defined solely in terms of a set of values and a set of operations on that data type. Each ADT operation is defined by its inputs and outputs.

Data Structures

A data structure is the physical implementation of an ADT. Each operation associated with the ADT is implemented by one or more subroutines or methods in the implementation. Data structure usually refers to an organization for data in main memory. Data items have both a logical and a physical form. Logical form is the definition of the data item within an ADT. Physical form is an implementation of the data item within a data structure.

1.2. A Data Structure Development Model

Algorithms and Programs

An algorithm a method, recipe, or a process followed to solve a problem. An algorithm takes the input to a problem and transforms it to the output.

Properties of an algorithm are:
- It must be correct.
- It must be composed of a series of concrete steps.
- There can be no ambiguity as to which step will be performed next.
- It must be composed of a finite number of steps.
- It must terminate.

A computer program is an instance, or concrete representation, for an algorithm in some programming language.

A node is the smallest addressable unit in a structure. Examples of nodes are detailed in Figure 1.

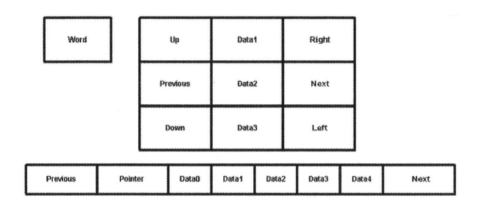

Figure 1. Examples of Nodes

A set of nodes with a set of physical operations defined on the nodes is a data structure. A Data Structure Model (DSM) is defined with a set of nodes and a set of operations on the nodes implemented as constructors and methods in a Java class. The Java class List.java implements operations for data structures. The class List.java is detailed in Appendix A. The DSM is implemented with algorithms embedded in the List.java class. The Java Programming language is used in this text to operate the data structure model paradigm. The DSM is detailed in Figure 2.

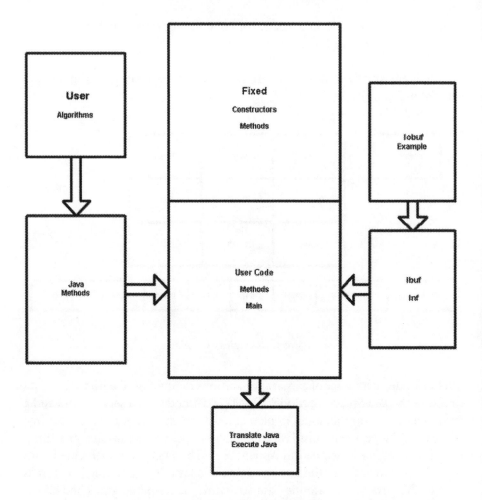

Figure 2. Data Structure Model

1.3. The Use of Java

Input and Output

Most applications require input and output. There are many ways to input and out data in Java. In this text we are using Java, so a limited amount of input and output is required to operate the data structure paradigm. An input and output resource example is detailed in Appendix B. Ibuf and Inf methods may be inserted into List.java to perform input for the data structure paradigm. Output may be implemented with the Java standard JOptionPane.

All data structures are implemented by inserting the methods Ibuf and Inf into the Java class List.java. Write a main and Java methods using the List.java constructors and methods, insert them into List.java, compile, and execute List.java. The methods Ibuf and Inf are methods detailed in Appendix B. A program segment of List.java after the insertion of Ibuf and Inf Methods for input is detailed in Figure 3.

```
// ************************************************************
// Insert User Java methods and Java public static void main
// ************************************************************
// Setup File Reference Handle
//-------------------------------------------
private BufferedReader Ibuf (String fileName)
throws java.io.IOException
  {
  // Set up the basic input stream.
  FileReader fr = new FileReader(fileName);
  // Buffer the input stream.
  BufferedReader br = new BufferedReader(fr);
  return br;
  } // End Ibuf


//-------------------------------------------
// Input a Data Item
//-------------------------------------------
public static String Inf (BufferedReader br)
throws java.io.IOException
{String inval;
  if ((inval = br.readLine())!= null)
    {
    return inval;
    } else return null;

} // End Inf
```

Figure 3. User List.java Input Program Segment

1.4. Exercises

1. Define data structures.

2. Define algorithm.

3. Describe the data structure model (DSM).

4. Describe the role of the Java programming language in the DSM.

5. Describe the methods in List.java.

2

Analysis Tools

In the introduction a definition of algorithm was detailed. Many techniques are used to write algorithms. Algorithms are sometimes called pseudo code. A heuristic for writing an algorithm is to use statements that approximate the statements in a target language. That is to say, use statements that are as-close-as possible to the language in which the algorithm will be coded as a program. The coding of an algorithm in a particular programming language is a program. The design phase of a problem produces an algorithm. The implementation phase produces a program for the designed algorithm. The best algorithm is determined with a thrall analysis of each step or set of steps. The basic science used in the analysis of algorithms involves mathematics and statistics.

2.1. A Mathematical Review

The analysis of algorithms requires the use of mathematics and statistics to estimate resources to measure the performance of algorithms. In this section, we summarize some of the fundamental concepts from discrete mathematics that will be used in several of our discussions.

2.1.1. Logarithms and Exponents

In the analysis of data structures and algorithms we use logarithms and exponents, expressed as

$\quad$ $Log_b a = c$ $\quad\quad$ if $a = b^c$, where $b = 2$ for the natural logarithm.

There are a number of rules for logarithms and exponents, including the following:

Let a, b, and c be positive real numbers. We have:

$\quad$ 1. $\log_b ac = \log_b a + \log_b c$

$\quad$ 2. $\log_b a/c = \log_b a - \log_b c$

3. $\log_b a^c = c\log_b a$
4. $\log_b a = (\log_c a) / \log_c b$
5. $b^{\log_c a} = a^{\log_c b}$
6. $(b^a)^c = b^{ac}$
7. $b^a b^c = b^{a+c}$
8. $b^a / b^c = b^{a-c}$

The value of a logarithm is a floating point number. The running time of an algorithm is expressed as an integer. Floor and ceiling functions are used to convert floating point numbers to integers.

$\lfloor x \rfloor$ = the largest integer less than or equal to x.

$\lceil x \rceil$ = the smallest integer greater than or equal to x.

2.1.2. Summation

The summation is used in the analysis of data structures and algorithms, which is defined as follows:

$$\sum_{i=t}^{n} f(i) = f(t) + f(t+1) + f(t+2) + \ldots + f(n).$$

A summation that often arises in data structure and algorithm analysis is the geometric summation. For any integer $n \geq 0$ and real number $0 < a \neq 1$, consider

$$\sum_{i=0}^{n} a^i = 1 + a + a^2 + \ldots + a^n = (1 - a^{n+1}) / (1 - a)$$

The largest integer that can be represented in binary notation using n bits is

$$1 + 2 + 4 + 8 + \ldots + 2^{n-1} = 2^n - 1.$$

Another summation often arises in the analysis of loops in cases where the number of operations performed inside the loop increases by a fixed or constant amount is

$$\sum_{i=1}^{n} i = 1 + 2 + 3 + \ldots + (n - 2) + (n - 1) + n.$$

2.1.3. Induction

The principle of finite induction is used in the analysis of data structure and algorithms. Most performance measures involving run time or a space bound involves an integer parameter n. Let there be associated with each positive integer n a proposition P(n) which is either true or false. If, firstly P(1) is true, and secondly, foe all k, P(k) implies P(k + 1), then P(n) is true for all positive integers n.

Show by induction that

$$\sum_{i=1}^{n} i = n(n + 1) / 2 .$$

Base case: n = 1. 1(1 + 1)/2 = 1.
Induction step: n ≥ 2. Assume the claim is true for k < n.

$$\sum_{i=1}^{k} i = k(k + 1) / 2 .$$

Consider n.

$$\sum_{i=1}^{n} i = n + \sum_{i=1}^{n-1} i.$$

By the induction hypothesis with k = n - 1, then

$$\sum_{i=1}^{n} i = n + (n - 1)n / 2,$$

which we can simplify as

$$n + (n - 1)n / 2 = (2n + n^2 - n) / 2 = (n^2 + n) / 2 = n(n + 1) / 2 .$$

The justification is true.

2.2. Asymptotic Notation

Order of magnitude analysis requires a number of mathematical definitions and theorems. The most basic concept is commonly termed big-O.

Suppose that f(n) and g(n) are nonnegative functions of n. Then we say that f(n) is O(g(n)) provided that there are constants C > 0 and N > 0 such that for all n > N, f(n) ≤ Cg(n). A function f is big-O of a function g if we find specific constants C and N for which the inequality holds.

Big-O expresses an upper bound on the growth rate of s function, for sufficiently large values of n.

Big-O Theorems: For all the following theorems, assume that f(n) is a function of n that C is an arbitrary constant.
1. C is O(1)

2. A polynomial is O(the term containing the highest power of n)
   $f(n) = 10n^4 + 8n^2 + 13n + 68$ is $O(10n^4)$
3. $Cf(n)$ is $O(f(n))$ (constant coefficients can be dropped)
   $g(n) = 10n^4$ is $O(n^4)$
4. If $f(n)$ is $O(g(n))$ and $g(n)$ is $O(h(n))$ then $f(n)$ is $O(h(n))$. (transitivity)
   $f(n) = 10n^4 + 8n^2 + 13n + 68$ is $O(n^4)$
5. Each of the following functions is big-O of its successors:
   C ; $\log_b (n)$, where $b = 2$; n; nlog(n); n^2; n to higher powers; 2^n; 3^n; larger constants to the nth power; n!; n^n
   $f(n) = 8n\log(n)$ is $O(n\log(n))$ and $O(n^2)$ and $O(2^n)$
6. In general, $f(n)$ is big-O of the dominant term of $f(n)$, where "dominant" may be determined from Theorem 5.
   $f(n) = 10n^2 + 8n \log (n) + 13n + 68$ is $O(n^2)$
   $g(n) = 21n^4 + 3^n + 350$ is $O(3^n)$
   $h(n) = 11n(n + \log (n))$ is $O(n^2)$
7. For any base b, $\log_b (n)$ is $O(\log (n))$.

Big-Theta is the lower bound on the growth of a function.

Suppose that $f(n)$ and $g(n)$ are nonnegative functions of n. Then we say that $f(n)$ is $\Omega(g(n))$ provided that there are constants $C > 0$ and $N > 0$ such that for all $n > N$, $f(n) \geq Cg(n)$. Big-Ω expresses a lower bound on the growth rate of a function, for sufficiently large values of n.

Finally, we may have two functions that grow at essentially the same rate. Suppose that $f(n)$ and $g(n)$ are nonnegative functions of n. Then we say that $f(n)$ is $\theta(g(n))$ provided that $f(n)$ is $O(g(n))$ and also that $f(h)$ is $\Omega(g(n))$.

2.3. Asymptotic Analysis

Suppose two algorithms solving the same problem are analyzed. Algorithm A has a running time of $\Theta(n)$ and Algorithm B has a running time of $\Theta(n^2)$. Which algorithm is better?

We need a parametric analysis over the range of n to determine the best algorithm under various conditions. Consider the asymptotic growth rate of several functions. The functions are $\log (n)$, $\log^2 (n)$, $(n)^{1/2}$, n, n log (n), n^2, n^3, and 2^n.
Data for these functions are detailed in Figure 4. Algorithm A is better than Algorithm B from an analysis of the data in Figure 4.

n	log n	n	n log n	n^2	n^3	2^n
1	0	1	0	1	1	2.E+00
10	3	10	33	100	1000	1.E+03
20	4	20	86	400	8000	1.E+06
30	5	30	147	900	27000	1.E+09
40	5	40	213	1600	64000	1.E+12
50	6	50	282	2500	125000	1.E+15
60	6	60	354	3600	216000	1.E+18
70	6	70	429	4900	343000	1.E+21
80	6	80	506	6400	512000	1.E+24
90	6	90	584	8100	729000	1.E+27
100	7	100	664	10000	1000000	1.E+30

Figure 4. Asymptotic Rate of Growth

2.4. Statistical Measures

In the analysis of data structures and algorithms some performance measures are defined in terms of the mean of observations. In other cases, measures are defined by approximating statistical distributions.

The arithmetic mean, or mean, of a set of observations is defined to be the sum of the observations divided by the total number of observations.

$$y^* = \left(\sum_{i=1}^{n} y_i\right) / 2$$

The mean for n observations is y^*. Additional statistical measures are detailed in [1].

2.5. Analysis of Algorithms

Coding an algorithm in a high level language, compiling the code, and executing the code with a unit cost defined on operations is accurate. This method required detail knowledge on the intermediate forms of the high level language and the environment in which it is to run.

We perform our analysis directly on the algorithm or pseudo-code. The pseudo code is independent from the high level programming language. Define a set of primitive operations that are independent of the programming language. Define measures on the operations in the pseudo-code. Primitive operations are detailed in Figure 5.

- Assigning a value to a variable
- Calling a method
- Performing an arithmetic operation
- Comparing two numbers
- Indexing into an array
- Following an object reference
- Processing a link operation
- Converting a recursive function into an equivalent non-recursive function.
- Returning from a method

Figure 5. Primitive Operations in Pseudo-Codes

Important measures of algorithms are best, average, and worst performance. The best performance is the minimum measure for the pseudo-code. Average performance is obtained by measuring the pseudo-code for a set of cases and applying the statistical computation in Figure 4. The worst performance measure is the maximum measure for the pseudo-code.

2.6. Exercises

1. Prove by induction for all $n \geq 0$,

$$\sum_{i=1}^{n} i(i + 1) / 2 = n(n + 1)(n + 2) / 6.$$

2. Write an algorithm to find the largest element in a set containing n entries. How many comparisons of elements does your algorithm do in the worst case? Execute your algorithm for several cases and calculate the average number of comparisons to find an element. What is the best case?

3. Use justification to show that $40n_3 + 10n \log n + 10$ is $O(n^3)$.

3

Stacks, Queues and Deques

The stack, queue, and deque linear structures are allocated using the sequential-allocation method of storage. These structures are accessed with sequential methods. In Chapter 4 we detail linked-allocation and linked access methods for stacks and queues.

3.1. Stacks

One of the most important linear structures of variable size is the stack. In this structure, we are allowed to delete an element from and add an element to occur only at one end. The addition operation is referred to as "push," and the deletion operation as "pop." The most and least accessible elements in a stack are known as the top and bottom of the stack, respectively. Since insertion and deletion operations are performed at the end of a stack, the element can only be removed in the opposite order from that in which they were added to the stack. This is referred to as the discipline, and is the last item inserted is the first item deleted (LIFO). A stack is detailed in Figure 6.

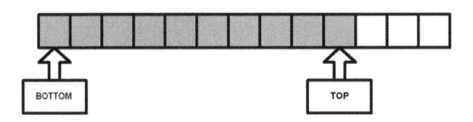

Figure 6. Linear Stack

Algorithm P inserts an element K into a stack S.

Algorithm P. Push an Element K Into a Stack S.
The stack index is TOP. S has n available slots to store elements.
P1. [Overflow: Is the stack full?] if TOP ≥ n {print overflow message; exit;}
P2. [Increment TOP] TOP = TOP + 1;
P3. [Insert element into the stack.] S[TOP] = K; exit;

Algorithm D deletes an element from the stack S and returns the element deleted in a variable K.

Algorithm D. Pop an Element K From a Stack S
The stack index is TOP.
D1. [Underflow: Is an element in the stack?] if TOP ≤ 0 {print underflow message; exit;}
D2. [Un-stack an element or POP the stack.] K = S[TOP];
D3. [Decrement the stack index.] TOP = TOP − 1; exit;

3.2. Queues

Another important linear structure of variable size is the queue. A queue permits deletions at one end and additions at the other. The information is processed in the same order as it was received. The discipline is first item in is the first item out (FIFO) or a first-come, first-served (FCFS) operation. This type of structure is called a queue. Items are inserted into the rear and deletions are taken from the front. A queue is detailed in Figure 7.

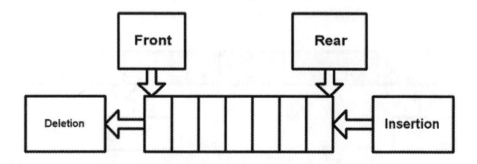

Figure 7. Linear Queue

Algorithm I inserts an element K into a queue Q.

Algorithm I. Insert an Element K into a Queue Q
Given values indexes F for front and R for rear elements of queue Q. Initially F and R have been set to a value of zero. There are slots for n elements in the queue.
I1. [Overflow: Is Q full?] if $R \geq n$ {print overflow message; exit;}
I2. [Increment the rear index] $R = R + 1$;
I3. [Insert the element K into the queue.] $Q[R] = K$;
I4. [Is the front index F properly set?] if $F = 0$ {F = 1; exit}

Algorithm J. deletes an element from the queue and returns it in K.

Algorithm J. Delete an Element From a Queue Q
The element deleted from the queue is stored in K.
J1. [Underflow: Is the queue empty?] if $F = 0$ {print underflow message; exit;}
J2. [Delete an element from the queue.] $K = Q[F]$;
J3. [Increment the front queue index.] $F = F + 1$; exit;

3.3. Deques

A deque is a special queue in which insertions and deletions are made from either the front or the rear of the queue. Operations on a deque are insert front, insert rear, delete front, and delete rear.

4

Lists

Instead of keeping a linear list in sequential memory locations, we can make use of a much more flexible scheme in which each node contains a link to the next node of the list. Define a variable whose content is the address or index of another location called a link variable or a pointer. Define a pointer to the linked allocation with a linked variable AVAIL. A linked allocation is detailed in Figure 8.

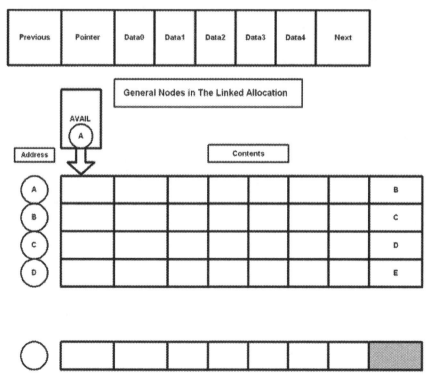

Figure 8. Linked Allocation With an Available Storage Pointer

In Figure 8, A, B, C, D, and E are arbitrary locations in memory, and shaded node is the null link. The link variable AVAIL points to the first node in the structure. The Next node of the structure contains the address or index to the next node in the structure. Other pointer nodes in the structure are Previous and Pointer. Data are stored as objects in the nodes Data0, Data1, ..., and Data4.

In a list processing (LISP) system the available storage pool is linked as the Next node is linked in Figure 8. A link variable points to the top of the storage pool. System operations are available to get a node from the pool, return a node to the pool, connect nodes using the link or Next node content, store data in nodes, retrieve data from nodes, and move from one node to another node.

Define and Allocate a List Node

The List.Java class in Appendix A details operations to setup and operate list using Java. The ListNode constructor is used to define and allocate a list node. Define and allocate called IT and set the link nodes to null.

  ListNode IT = new ListNode (null);

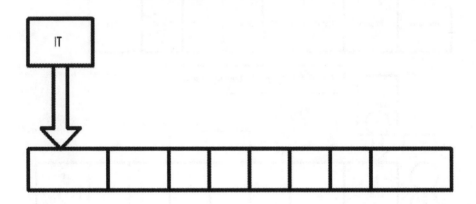

Figure 9. A Node Pointed to by IT

Store Data in a List Node

Store an integer IG in the node pointed to by IT. First convert the integer IG to an object IGG.

  Integer IGG = new Integer (IG);

Store the object IGG in Data0 using the infoi method of the List class..

  infoi (IT, IGG, 0);

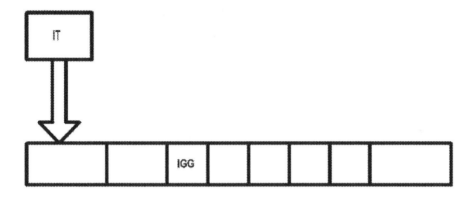

Figure 10. Store a Data Object into a Node Pointed to by IT

Define and Allocate a List Node and Store Data

Generate a another node and point to it with NX.
      ListNode NX = new ListNode (null);
Store an integer IK in the node pointed to by NX. First convert the integer IK to an object IKK.
      Integer IKK = new Integer (NX);
Store the object IKK in Data0 using the infoi method of the List class.
      infoi (NX, IKK, 0);

Connect two List Nodes Using the Next and Previous Pointers

We have two nodes, one pointed to by IT and the second pointed to by NX. Connect the list node pointed to by NX to the node pointed to by IT. The method in the List.java class that connects nodes using the Next node is called CONS.
      CONS (IT, NX);
Connect the node using the Previous node or backward pointer with the LCONS method from the class List.java.
      LCONS (NX, IT);

Move from Node-to-Node on a List

We have a double linked list pointed to by IT. To move from node-to-node on the list Next pointer use a method from the class List.java called CDR. The method CDR has a ListNode type.
      ListNode GR = CDR (IT);

To move from node-to-node on the list Previous pointer, use a method from the class List.java called LCDR. The method CDR has a ListNode type.

ListNode GR = LCDR (IT);

Retrieve Data from a List Node

The last basic operation is to retrieve data from a node pointed to by a link variable. Retrieve the data from the list pointed to by IT. Use the List.java class method info to retrieve data0 from a list node. The method info has an object type.

Object RE = info (IT, 0);

4.1. Single Linked List

We have operations defined on a list data structure in the List.java class. Algorithm L details the steps to setup a single-linked list using the List.java class.

Algorithm L. Append a Node to a Single Linked List

Input parameters to this algorithm are a pointer to the end of the list IL and string data K to be stored in the appended node. This algorithm has a ListNode type. The pointer to the node appended to the list is returned.

L1. [Define and allocate a new node to be appended to the end of the existing list pointed to by IL.]
ListNode IE = new ListNode (null);
L2. [Convert the data to be stored into the appended node to an object. A String is an object in Java. This conversion is performed on a String to point out the language construct used in the conversion process. Convert the String K to an integer KI. Convert KI to an Object KJ.]
KI = Integer.ParseInt (K); Integer KJ = new Integer (KI);
L3. [Store the object in the new node that will be appended to the list.]
infoi (IE, KJ, 0);
L4. [Connect the New Node to the List]
CONS (IL, IE);
L5. [Return the pointer to last node in the list. This is the pointer to the node appended to the list.]
return IE;

Java Method for Algorithm L

```
public ListNode L (ListNode GN, String K)
{ ListNode GNN = GN;
  int KI;
  // Define and allocate a new list node.
  ListNode IE = new ListNode (null);
  // Convert the string to an integer;
  KI = Integer.ParseInt (K);
  // Convert the integer to an object.
  Integer KJ = new Integer (KI);
  // Store the data in Data0 of the new node.
  infoi (IE, KJ, 0);
  // Connect the new node to the list.
  CONS (GNN, IE);
  // Return the pointer to the last node in the list.
  return IE;
} // End L
```

A single linked list pointed to by a link variable IT is detailed in Figure 11.

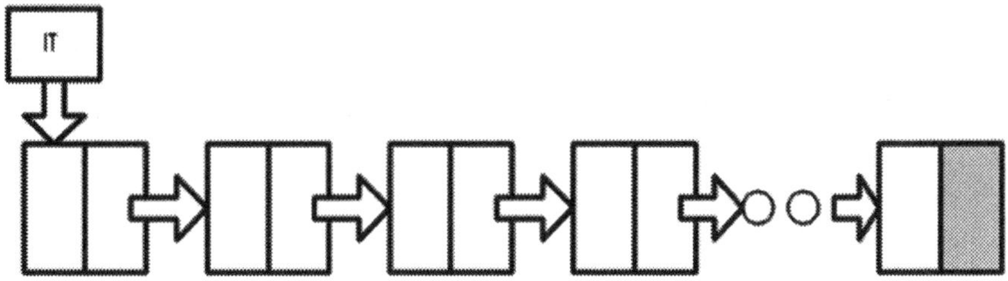

Figure 11. Single Linked List

List needs space for the objects actually on the list. Lists storage space is bounded by the number of objects on a linked list, as long as there is an available storage pool of memory space. The amount of space required for a linked list is $O(n)$.

A single linked list requires that a pointer be added to every list node. If the object size is small, then the overhead for links can be a significant fraction of the total storage.

Let n be the number of objects currently in the list. Define P to be the size of a pointer in storage units, and E the size of an object in storage units. The amount of space required for the linked list is n(P + E). In general, the linked implementation requires less space than an array-based implementation when relatively few elements are in the list. An array-based implementation requires that space be allocated for the worse case of the number of objects to be stored in the array-based list. In general, the space allocated for an array-based list implementation is not releases or freed for other component of the life of a process.

As a rule of thumb, linked lists are better when implementing lists whose number of elements varies widely or is unknown.

In the normal linked list, the next field of the last element stores the value null. Storing a pointer to the first element in the list in the last pointer node of the list creates a circular
list. A circular single linked list is detailed in Figure 12.

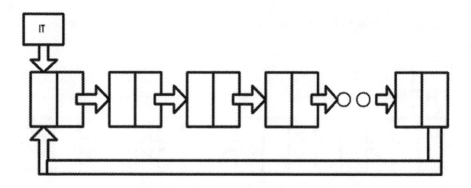

Figure 12. Circular Single Linked List

Display the Data in a List

Given a pointer to a list, retrieve the data from each node and output it to an output device. Algorithm D details the steps to use a pointer to a list to retrieve data from the nodes. The algorithm moves or walks from node-to-node using info to retrieve data from each node.

Algorithm D. Display Information in a List
The information is stored in a list pointed to by IK.

P1. [Initialize a Temporary Pointer to the List] ListNode IQ; IQ = IK; Object out;

P2. [Repeat to P4. Test For a List or the Last Node] if (IQ == Null) { print ("All Information Displayed"); terminate;}

P3. [Display the Information] out = info (IQ, 0); print (out);

P4. [Move to the Next Node in the List] IQ = CDR (IQ);

Java Method for Algorithm D

```
public void D (ListNode IR)
{ ListNode IRR = IR;
  ListNode IQ;
  Object out;
  IQ = IRR;
  while (IQ!= null)
  { // Retrieve the data from Data0 of the list node.
    out = info (IQ);
    // Output the list node data.
    JOptionPane.showMessageDialog(null,"List Node Data: "+out.toString ());
    // Move or walk to the next node of the list.
    IQ = CDR (IQ);
  } // End D
```

Code Segment to Load Data into a Single Linked List

This Java code segment is designed to be inserted into the List.java class in the user area using the DSM defined in Figure 2. Insert the Java method L into the user area of the List.java class.

```
public static void main(String args[])
throws java.io.IOException
{ // Delcare Variables
  String foo = "AA";
  public int sw = 0;
  int tmo = 0;
  ListNode TA;
  ListNode IT;
  // Define a Reference Variable to the Container
  List  DL = new List ();
  BufferedReader tk;
  // Set the Path and Input File Name
  String FName = "C:\\spring2004\\csc251\\INFO.DAT";
```

```
// Setup file reference handle
tk = DL.Ibuf(FName);
// Setup the first node of the list with a pointer IT
foo = DL.Inf (tk);
// Get a node and point to it with IA.
ListNode IA = new ListNode (null);
// Convert the data to an integer;
tmo = Integer.ParseInt (foo);
// Convert the integer to an object.
Integer JJ = new Integer (tmo);
// Store the object in Data0 of the new list node.
DL.infoi (IA, JJ, 0);
// Store the pointer in TA for use in loading the file data.
TA = IA;
// Save the pointer to the list.
IT = IA;
// Read an Input Data Items One-at-a-Time from the input file
while (foo!= null)
{ // Input Data and Return String Data Value
  foo = DL.Inf (tk);
  // Check for null.
  if (foo == null) break;
  // Store a data item in the list and append to the list pointed to by IT.
  TA = DL.L (TA, foo);
  } // End while
// Close the Input File
tk.close();
// Display the data in the list using algorithm D in the list pointed to by IT..
DL.D (IT);
// Terminate Program
System.exit(0);
} // End Method main
```

Search Linked List

Algorithm S. Search for An Object K in a List

Find an item K in a list pointed to by IK and return the pointer to the node. Return a pointer of null for an unsuccessful search. Algorithm S has a ListNode type. Input to the search algorithm are the input key K and the pointer IK to the list to be searched.

S1. [Initialize a temporary pointer to the list.] ListNode IQ; IQ = IK;
  Object out;
S2. [Repeat to S5. Test for a list or the last node.]
  if (IQ == Null) { print ("Search Failed.");
    return (null); terminate;}
S3. [Get the information Data0 from the node.] out = info(IQ, 0);
S4. [Test for K] if (K == out.toString ())
      {print ("Found"); return IQ; Stop;}
S5. [Move to the next node in the list.] IQ = CDR(IQ);

4.2. Double Linked List

A double linked list is setup by inserting an invocation of the LCONS method in step L4 of algorithm L.
  LCONS (IE, IL);

A double-linked list requires that a pointer to the previous node and a pointer to the next node be added to every list node. If the object size is small, then the overhead for links can be a significant fraction of the total storage. The storage for links is twice that of a single-linked list.

Let n be the number of objects currently in the list. Define P to be the size of a pointer in storage units, and E the size of an object in storage units. The amount of space required for the double linked list is $n(2P + E)$. In general, the linked implementation requires less space than an array-based implementation when relatively few elements are in the list. An array-based implementation requires that space be allocated for the worse case of the number of objects to be stored in the array-based list. In general, the space allocated for an array-based list implementation is not releases or freed for other component of the life of a process. More storage is used for links in a double linked list than a single linked list. A double linked list is detailed in Figure 13.

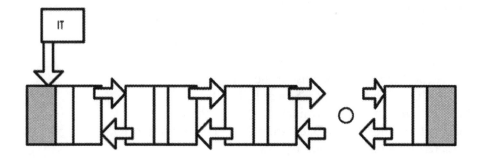

Figure 13. Double Linked List

Algorithms that require movement in the previous and next direction are simple using a double linked list. Trailing pointers are required in single linked list to move backward in the list. This complicates the single linked list algorithms. The entire single linked list must be traversed form the beginning over and over again to set the trailing pointer.

As a rule of thumb, double linked lists are better when implementing lists whose number of elements varies widely or is unknown.

In the normal double linked list, the next field of the last node and the previous field of the first node stores the value null. Store a pointer to the first node in the list in the last pointer node of the list, and store a pointer in the previous node of the first node of the list to the last node of the list creates a circular double linked list. A circular double linked list is detailed in Figure 14.

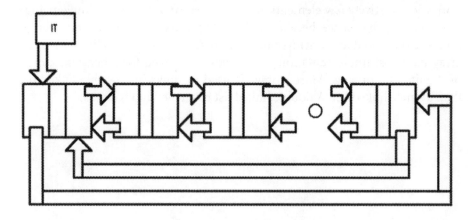

Figure 14. Circular Double Linked List

Delete a Node From a Double Linked List

Algorithm V. Delete a Node From a Double Link List

Delete the node pointer to by ID from a double linked list.
V1. [Initialize temporary variables.] ListNode IL; ListNode IR;
V2. [Get the right or next and left or previous link from the node.]
IL = LCDR(ID); IR = CDR(ID);
V3. [Reconnect the list after the node has been deleted.]
CONS (IR, IL); LCONS (IL, IR); terminate;

Insert into a Double Linked List

Algorithm W. Insert a Node to the Right of a Node in a Double Link List

Insert a node to the right of a node pointer to by ID in a double link list.
W1. [Initialize temporary variables.] ListNode IR = Null;
W2. [Get the right or next link from the node.]
if (ID.next!= Null) IR = CDR (ID); else IR = Null;
W3. [Get a node to insert into the list.]
ListNode IN = new ListNode (null);
W4. [Reconnect the list nodes.] CONS (ID, IN);
LCONS (IN, ID); CONS (IN, IR);
if (IR!= Null) LCONS (IR, IN); terminate;

Display the Data in a Double Linked List

Algorithm U. Display Information in a Double Link List

The information is stored in a list pointed to by IK.
U1. [Initialize a temporary pointer to the list.] ListNode IQ = IK;
U2. [Repeat to U4. Test for a list or the last node.]
if (IQ == Null) { print ("All Information Displayed"); terminate;}
U3. [Display the information.] K = info(IQ, 0); print (K.toString ());
U4. [Move to the next node in the list.] IQ = CDR(IQ);

4.3. Exercises

1. Use the DSM to implement an algorithm as a method or set of methods to setup a double linked list pointed to by a linked variable P to simulate task in an operating system. Load the task arrival times from a hard disk file called TASK.DAT into the list with priorities assigned to each arrival from a uniform

random distribution. Example int prority = (int)(1 + (Math.random () *5)). Assign a positive integer name to each task. The arrival time data stored as one number per record in TASK.DAT are 2, 8, 20, 10, 6, 12, 50, 4, 1, 30. TASK.DAT has 10 data items; however, the input must be designed for an unknown number of items. Hint: use a while statement and the fact that Java read a null as the end of file with BufferReader input. Display the data in the double linked list pointed to by P. The data are to be displayed in a graphics user interface (GUI) message box are task arrival times, task priority, and task name.

2. Use the double linked list from problem 1 pointed to by P, and implement an algorithm as methods to implement a server with time slices and priorities drawn from uniform random distributions. The server serves one task in each pass through the double linked list. A pass is defined as a cycle through the double linked list to find a task with a priority nearest the one drawn from the uniform distribution by the server. The server decrements a Task arrival time by the time slice drawn form a uniform distribution by the server with the nearest priority on each simulation cycle. Difference = Current Task Arrival Time – Current Server Time Slice. At each cycle of the simulation the task name, time, priority, server time slice, and server priority are printed in a GUI dialog box. If the server Difference is zero or less delete the Task from the list. Otherwise, the Task new arrival time Difference and the current server priority time is used to update the current Task list node. The algorithm terminates when the list is empty.

5

Linked Stacks and Queues

The direction of links for both the stack and queue are such as to facilitate easy insertion and deletion of nodes. A node can be added at the top or deleted one from the top. Also, a node can be added at the rear and both addition and deletion can be performed at the front, for a queue we normally would not wish to add nodes at the front.

5.1. Linked Stacks

We have already seen how to represent stacks and queues sequentially. Such a representation proved efficient if we had only one stack or one queue. However, when several stacks and queues co-exist, there was no efficient way to represent them sequentially.

The operation of adding an object to the front of a linked list is quite similar to that of pushing an object onto a stack. In both cases, a new object is added as the only immediately accessible item in a collection. A stack can be accessed only through its top object, and a lists can be accessed only from the pointer to its first object. Similarly, the operation of removing the first object from a linked list is analogous to popping a stack. In both cases, the only immediately accessible object of a collection is removed from that collection, and the next object becomes immediately accessible. We represent a linked stack by a linear linked list. A linked stack is detailed in Figure 15.

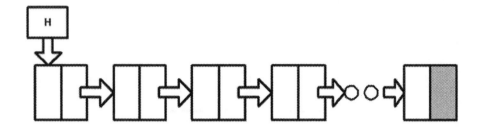

Figure 15. Linked Stack

Algorithm X details a push operation on a linked stack. Algorithm M details a pop operation on a linked stack.

Algorithm X. Push Information on a Link Stack

Push a node on a link stack pointed to by H. The beginning of the stack is pointed to by IB. The information for the stack is in K.
X1. [Initialize. H points to the top of the stack or the front of the list.]
X2. [Get a node and save the pointer in IG. The stack boundary is controlled by the number of nodes in the pool.] ListNode IG = new ListNode (null);
X3. [Push on the node onto the stack.] CONS(H, IG);
X4. [Set the stack pointer.] H = IG;
X5. [Convert the Data to an object. Store the information in Data0.]
    KL = Integer.ParseInt (K);
    Integer KN = new Integer (KL); infoi(H, K, 0); terminate;

Algorithm M. Pop Information From a Link Stack

IB points to the beginning of the stack. Pop a node from a link stack pointed to by H. The information form the stack is stored in K. The algorithm result has an object type.
M1. [Test for an empty stack.]
    if (H == Null) { print ("The Stack is Empty"); terminate;}
M2. [Pop the stack and remove the node from the link stack.]
    ListNode TK = IB; ListNode TM;
    while (TK!= H) {TM = TK; TK = CDR (TK);} IG = H; H = TM;
M3. [Return the information from the stack node Data0.]
    K = info (IG, 0); return K;
M4. [Terminate] stop;

5.2. Linked Queues

Objects are deleted from the front of a queue and inserted at the rear. Let the list pointer that points to the first object of a list represent the front of the queue. Another pointer to the last object of the list represents the front of the queue. A linked queue is detailed in Figure 16.

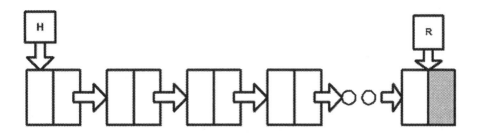

Figure 16. Linked Queue

Algorithm Q details a linked queue push operation. Algorithm N details a linked queue pop operation.

Algorithm Q. Push Information on a Link Queue

Push a node on a link queue pointed to by H. The information for
the queue is in K. R is the rear pointer to the queue. R is set
the first time an item is pushed on to the queue.
Q1. [Get a node and save the pointer in IG. The queue boundary is controlled
    by the number of nodes in the storage pool.]
    ListNode IG = new ListNode (null);
Q2. [Push on the new node onto the queue. Point the front pointer
    to the queue.] if (CDR(H) == Null) R = H; CONS (H, IG); H = IG;
Q4. [Convert the data to an object, Store the information in Data0.]
    KL = Integer.ParseInt (K); Integer GK = new Integer (KL);
    infoi(H, K, 0); terminate;

Algorithm N. Pop Information From a Link Queue

Pop a node from a link queue pointed to by a rear pointer R. The information
form the queue is stored in K. The output type for this algorithm is object.
N1. [Test for an empty queue.]

if (R == Null) {print ("The Queue is Empty"); terminate;}
N2. [Return the information from Data0. Point to the next node
in the queue.] K = info(R, 0); R = CDR(R); return K;
N3. [Terminate] stop;

5.3. Exercises

1. Use the DSM to implement an algorithm as a method or set of methods to setup a double linked queue with a front pointer F and a back pointer B. Implement a method to invoke the PoP method for the queue and display each data item in a GUI interface message box. Terminate the display when the queue is empty. Load the arrival time from a hard disk file called CAR.DAT into the queue. The data stored as one number per record in CAR.DAT are 2, 8, 20, 10, 6, 12, 50, 4, 1, 30. CAR.DAT has 10 data items; however, the input must be designed for an unknown number of items. Assign a positive integer name to each arrival drawn from a uniform random distribution.

2. Load the data in problem 1 into the double linked queue. Use the double linked queue from problem 3 pointed to by F and B to implement an algorithm as methods to implement a server with time slices drawn from a uniform random distribution. On each simulation cycle the server pops the queue, decrements the car arrival time (New Arrival Time = Current Car Arrival Time − Server Time Slice), if a car new arrival time is zero or less delete the car from the queue, else if the car new arrival time is greater than zero push the car new arrival time with its attributes on the queue. Count the number of simulation cycles per car, number of cars in the queue, and the total number of simulation cycles. At each cycle of the simulation the car name, current arrival time, server time slice, simulation cycles per car, and cumulative simulation cycles are displayed in a GUI dialog box. The algorithm terminates when the queue is empty.

3. Use the DSM to implement an algorithm as a method or set of methods to setup a double linked stack pointed to by a linked variable B. Load the information from a hard disk file called STK.DAT into the stack. The data stored as one number per record in STK.DAT are 2, 260, 7, 4, 7, 3, 450, 700, 3, 88, 600, 6, 300, 100, 3, 6, 80, 50, 10. The number 3 is +; 4 is -; 6 is *; 7 is /, and 2 is =. STK.DAT has 19 data items; however, the input must be designed for an unknown number of items. Display the data in the double linked stack pointed to by B. The data are to be displayed in a graphics user interface (GUI) message box.
Note on triples:

Method to generate triples from the data in the input stack. Setup an array TMP of temporaries T1, T2, ..., T10. Implement a Triple Algorithm.

Algorithm G. Triple Generator
G1. [Initialize] i = -1; IP points to the input Stack. IQ points to the output stack.
G2. [Pop the input stack] while (IP!= 0) {   KP = Pop (IP);
G3. [Is this an Operator?] if (KP == Operator)
{ OP1 = Pop (IQ); IP2 = Pop (IQ);
//Generate a Triple
Trip [i+1][0] = KP; Trip [i+1][1] = OP1; Trip [i+1][2] = OP2;
//Push the temporary onto the output stack
i= i+1; Push (IQ, TMP [i]); } // End Operator
G4. [It is not an operator.] Push (IQ, KP);
} //End while on Input Stack
G5. [Output all Triples] for (j = 0; j <=i; ++j) print (Trip[j][0], Trip[j][1],Trip[j][2]);

4. Use the DSM to load the stack with the data and setup code from problem 5. Design and implement algorithms as methods to generate triples from the information in the stack. Post all the output in one GUI dialog box.

6

Binary Trees and Binary Search Trees

6.1. General Trees

A general tree T is a finite set of one or more nodes such that there is one designated node r, called the root of T, and the remaining nodes are partitioned into $n = 0$ disjoint subsets $T_1, T_2, \ldots, T_n$, each of which is a tree, and whose roots $r_1, r_2, \ldots, r_n$, respectively, are children of r. A general tree is detailed in Figure 17.

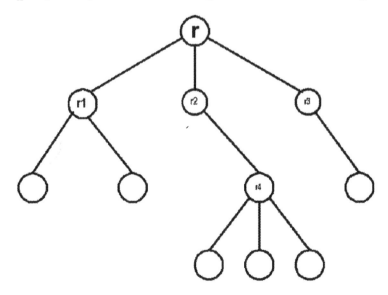

Figure 17. General Tree

It follows from our definition that every node of a tree is the root of some sub-tree contained in the whole tree. The number of subtrees of a node is called the degree of the node. A node of degree zero is called a terminal node or some-times a "leaf." A nonterminal node is often called a branch node. The level of a node with respect to T is defined by saying that the root has level 0, and other nodes have a level that is one higher than they have with respect to the subtree of the root, T_j which contains them.

The root in Figure 17 is r, and its three subtrees {r1}, {r2, r4}, and {r3}. The tree {r2} has node r as its root. Node r2 is on level 1 with respect to the whole tree, and it has one subtree {r4}. Therefore f2 has degree 1.

Standard terminology for tree structures is taken from the second form of family tree, the lineal chart: Each root is said to be the father of the roots of its subtree, and the latter are said to be brothers, and they are sons of their father. The root of the entire tree has no father, For example, in Figure 17, r4 has three sons.

6.2. Binary Trees

A binary tree is a finite set of elements that is either empty or contains a single element called the root of the tree and whose remaining elements are parti-tioned into disjoint subsets, each of which is itself a binary tree. These two sub-sets are called the left and right subtrees of the original tree. Each element of a binary tree is called a node of the tree. A binary tree is detailed in Figure 18.

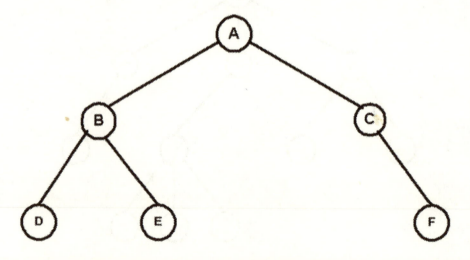

Figure 18. Binary Tree

The tree in Figure 18 consists of six nodes with A as its root. Its left subtree is rooted at B and its right subtree is rooted at C. This is indicated by the two branches emanating from A: to B on the left and to C on the right. The absence of a branch indicates an empty subtree. The binary trees rooted at D, E, and F have empty right and left subtrees.

If n1 is the root of a binary tree and n2 is the root of its left or right subtree, then n1 is said to be the father of n2 and n2 is said to be the left or right son of n1. A node that has no sons is called a leaf node. Node n1 is an ancestor of node n2 if n1 is either the father of n2 or the father of some ancestor of n2. A node n2 is a left descendant of node n1 if n2 is either the left son of n1 or a descendant of the left son of n1. A right descendant may be similarly defined. Two nodes are brothers if they are left and right sons of the same father.

The root of the tree has level 0 and the level of any other node in the tree is one more than the level of its father. For example, the binary tree of Figure 18, node B is at level 1 and F is at level 2. A complete binary tree of level n is one in which each node of level n is a leaf and in which each node of level less than n has nonempty left and right subtrees.

A linked binary tree pointed to by a link variable IT is detailed in Figure 19.

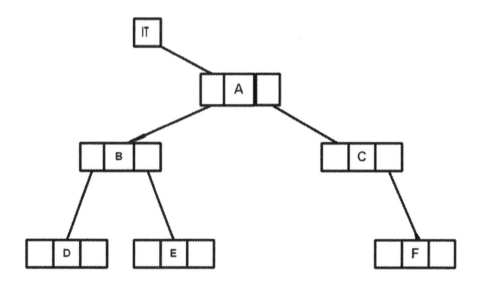

Figure 19. Linked Binary Tree

Binary Tree Traversals

One of the most common operations performed on tree structures is that of traversal. This is a procedure by which each node is processed exactly once in some systematic manner. This terminology was popularized by Knuth [3]. We can traverse a binary tree in three ways namely, in pretorder, in inorder, and in postorder. These traversals are defined with recursive definitions.

Preorder traversal
Process the root.
Traverse the left subtree in preorder.
Traverse the right subtree in preorder.

Inorder traversal
Traverse the left subtree in inorder.
Process the root node
Traverse the right subtree in inorder.

Postorder traversal
Traverse the left subtree in postorder
Traverse the right subtree in postorder.
Process the root node.

If a particular subtree is empty, the traversal is performed by doing nothing. In other words, a null subtree is considered to be fully traversed when it is encountered. The preorder, inorder, and postorder traversals of the binary tree in Figure 19 will process the nodes in the following order:

ABDECF   (preorder)
DBEACF   (inorder)
DEBFCA   (postorder)

These binary tree traversal definitions are implemented as non-recursive algorithms to improve the readers knowledge in list processing. Programming these algorithms will enhance the readers programming skills by operating close to the LISP paradigm. Algorithm F implements a binary tree preorder traversal. Algorithm H implements a binary tree inorder traversal. Algorithm G implements a binary tree postorder traversal.

Algorithm F. Traverse a Binary Tree in Preorder

Traverse a binary tree in preorder. Visit the root; Traverse the left subtree; Traverse the right subtree. T is a pointer to the binary tree. S is a double linked stack with pointer J.

F1. [Initialize.] ListNode J; ListNode P = T;
F2. [Is it a tree?] if (P == Null){print ("No tree."); Stop;}
F3. [Visit node, push pointer onto the stack. Move left. Repeat to F4.]
    print (info(P, 0)); J = Push(J, P); P=LCDR(P);
F4. [Repeat to F6 When P=Null. Subtree?]
    if (P == Null)
    {
F5. [Pop stack.] P = Pop(J); J = LCDR(J); if (J == NULL) {print("Complete");
    Terminate;}
F6. [Move Right.] P = CDR(P);
    }

Algorithm H. Traverse a Binary Tree in Inorder

Traverse a binary tree in postorder. Traverse the left subtree; Visit the root; Traverse the right subtree; . The pointer to the binary tree is T. A double linked stack is used with a pointer S to the top of the stack.

H1. [Initialize.] ListNode S; ListNode P; P = T;
    if (P == Null) {print ("No binary tree."); Terminate;}
H2. [Repeat to H4 Until P = Null for inner while. Continue to H7 for the outer while.]
    while (P!= Null) { while (P!= Null) {
H3. [Push the pointer P onto the stack. Store the pointer in the pointer node.]
    S= Push(S, P);
H4. [Move left.] P = LCDR(P);
    } // end inner while
H5. [Pop the stack into P.] if (S == NULL){ Terminate; }
                    else { P = Pop(S); S = LCDR(S);}
H6. [Visit P or get the object from Data0.] print (info(P, 0));
H7. [Move right.] P = CDR(P); } // end outer while

Algorithm G. Traverse a Binary Tree in Postorder

Traverse a binary tree in postorder. Traverse the left subtree; Traverse the right subtree; Visit the Root. T is a pointer to the binary tree. A stack is used with pointer J.

G1. [Initialize.] ListNode J; ListNode Q; ListNode P = T;
G2. [Is this a tree?] if (P == Null) {print("No binary tree."); Terminate;
G3. [Push the pointer onto the stack. Move left.]
   while (P!= null) { J = Push(J, P); P = LCDR(P);} // end while P!=
G4. [Pop the double linked stack.] if (J == NULL) { print("Complete");
   Terminate;}
   while (J!= null)
   { P = Pop(J);
     J = LCDR(J);
     if (Tago(J)!=null){ print(info(P, 0)); Tagi(J, null); J=LCDR(J); break;}
     if (CDR(P)!= null) {Push (J, P); P = LCDR(P); Tagi(J, 1)}
G5. [Move Right.]Q = P; P = CDR(P);
G6. [Right subtree?] if (P == Null) {print(info(Q)); break;}
G7. [Move left.] while (P!= null) { J = Push(J, P); P = LCDR(P);} // end while P!=
   } // end while J!=

Tago(J) return J.ptr;
Tagi(J, K) J.ptr = K;

6.3. Binary Search Trees

A binary search tree t is a binary tree; either it is empty or each node in the tree
contains an identifier and:

(i)   all identifiers in the left subtree of t are less (numerically or alpha-
      betically) than the identifier in the root node t;
(ii) all identifiers in the right subtree of t are greater than the identifier
      in the rootnode of t;
(iii) the left and right subtrees of t are also binary search trees.

For a given set of identifiers several binary search trees are possible. To determine whether an identifier x is present in a binary search tree, x is compared
with the root. If a is less than the identifier in the root, then the search continues in the left subtree; if x equals the identifier in the root, the search terminates successfully; otherwise the search continues in the right subtree. This is
formalized in algorithm S. A binary search tree is detailed in Figure 20.

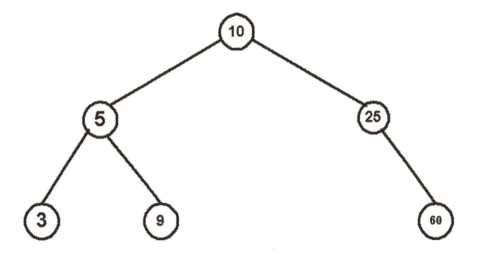

Figure 20. Binary Search Tree

In evaluating binary search trees, it is useful to add a null in the link fields of the terminal nodes. Every binary tree with n nodes has n + 1 null links. Nodes with null links are called external nodes. The nodes without null links are internal nodes. Each time a binary search tree is examined for an identifier which is not in the tree, the search terminates at an external or failure node. We define the external path length of a binary tree to be the sum over all external nodes of the lengths of the paths from the root to those nodes. An internal path length is defined to be the sum over all internal nodes of the lengths of the paths from the root to those nodes. For the tree of Figure 20 we obtain its internal path length, K, to be:

$$K = 0 + 2 + 1 + 2 = 5$$

Its external path length, E, is:

$$E = 3 + 2 + 3 = 8.$$

The internal and external path lengths of a binary tree with n internal nodes are related by the formula E = K + 2n. The worst case occurs when the tree is skewed. The value of K for a skewed tree is,

$$K = \sum_{i=0}^{n-1} i = n(n-1)/2.$$

The trees with minimal K must have as many internal nodes as close to the root as possible. The smallest value for K is

$$\sum_{i \le j \le n} \log_2 j = O(n \log_2 n).$$

Objects are loaded into a binary search tree with Algorithm B.

Load a Binary Search Tree

Algorithm B. Load A Binary Search Tree

Load any number of data items from a hard disk into a binary search tree. The pointer to the binary search tree is IT. The item to be loaded is stores in K.

B1. [Convert the string K to an integer. Check for the first node to store in the binary search tree.]

```
ListNode IH;
int X = Integer.ParseInt (K);
Integer W = new Integer (X);
if (sw == 0)
  { Listnode  IT;
    ListNode IG = new ListNode (null); infoi(IG, W, 0);
    IT = IG; sw = 1; return IT;
  }
```

B2. [Obtain the information from the tree node.]

```
ListNode IG = IT;
Object KL = info(IG, 0);
```

B3. [Determine the Subtree to insert a new node and store the object in Data0.]

B4. [Is it the left subtree?] if (W < = KL) { ListNode IQ = IG; IG = LCDR(IG); if (IG == Null)

```
{ //Store object in the Left subtree
```

B5. [Get a node to store the object in Data0.] ListNode IH = new ListNode (null);

B6. [Store the object in Data0.] infoi(IH, W, 0);

B7. [Connect the node to the binary search tree.] LCONS(IQ, IH); return IT;

```
  }
} // W <= KL
```

B8. [Is it the right subtree?] if (W > KL) { IQ = IG; IG = CDR(IG);
   if (IG == Null)
   { //Store object in the Right subtree.
B9. [Get a node to store the object in Data0.] ListNode IH = new ListNode(null);
B10. [Store the object in Data0.] infoi(IH, W, 0);
B11. [Connect the node to the binary search tree.] CONS(IQ, IH); return IT;
   }
  } // End if K L> W

Search a Binary Search Tree

If we traced the nodes visited on a search path for a key in a full binary search tree, we will probe exactly the same items that we would in conducting a binary search on a physically ordered array containing the same data. In this case, the search efficiency is $O(\log_2 n)$. Algorithm B details a search of a binary search tree.

Algorithm S. Search A Binary Search Tree

Search a binary search tree for a key M and return a pointer to the node. The pointer to the binary search tree is IT. This algorithm has a ListNode type.
S1. [Initialize.] ListNode IG = IT; Integer H= new Integer(M);
S2. [Obtain the information from the tree node.] while (IG!= null){
   Object K = info(IG, 0);
S3. [H = K?]if(H==K){ print("Key Found"); Stop;}
S4. [Look in the left subtree for the object.]
   if (K < H)
    { IG = LCDR(IG);
     if (IG == null)
      { print ("The object is not in the tree."); Terminate;
      }
    break;
    }
S5. [Look for the object in the right subtree.]
   if (K > H)
    { IG =CDR(IG);
     if (IG == null)
      { print ("The object is not in the tree."); Terminate;
      }
    break;
    }
  } // end while

6.4. Exercises

1. Use the DSM to implement an algorithm as a method or set of methods to setup a binary search tree pointed to by a linked variable T. Load the information from a hard disk file called BST.DAT into the binary search tree. The data stored as one number per record in BST.DAT are 3, 8, 20, 10, 6, 12, 50, 4, 1, 30, 2. BST.DAT has 11 data items; however, the input must be designed for an unknown number of items. Design and implement an algorithm as methods with post order traversal. Post all the output in one GUI dialog box.

2. Use the DSM to implement an algorithm as a method or set of methods to setup a binary search tree pointed to by a linked variable T. Load the information from a hard disk file called BST.DAT into the binary search tree. The data stored as one number per record in BST.DAT are 3, 8, 20, 10, 6, 12, 50, 4, 1, 30, 2. BST.DAT has 11 data items; however, the input must be designed for an unknown number of items. Design and implement an algorithm as methods with post order traversal and generate triples for the input. Post all the output in one GUI dialog box.

3. Use the DSM to implement an algorithm as a method or set of methods to setup a binary search tree pointed to by a linked variable T. Load the information from a hard disk file called BST.DAT into the binary search tree. The data stored as one number per record in BST.DAT are 3, 8, 20, 10, 6, 12, 50, 4, 1, 30, 2. BST.DAT has 11 data items; however, the input must be designed for an unknown number of items. Design and implement an algorithm as methods with preorder traversal. Post all the output in one GUI dialog box.

4. Use the DSM to implement an algorithm as a method or set of methods to setup a binary search tree pointed to by a linked variable T. Load the information from a hard disk file called BST.DAT into the binary search tree. The data stored as one number per record in BST.DAT are 3, 8, 20, 10, 6, 12, 50, 4, 1, 30, 2. BST.DAT has 11 data items; however, the input must be designed for an unknown number of items. Design and implement an algorithm as methods with inorder traversal. Post all the output in one GUI dialog box.

5. Prove that a binary tree with n nodes has exactly n + 1 null branches.

7

Hashing

We are given a key K, for a record and a key-to-address or index transformation, that generates an address or index used in the storage or retrieval of that record in a table. We use the term bucket as that area in a table where records are stored. The bucked size is the maximum number of records that can be contained in a bucket. A bucket can be thought of as being divided into slots. Each slot is designed to hold one data record. Therefore, the ratio of the active keys to the total slots available in all buckets is called the load factor.

A key-to-address transformation h(K), sometimes called a hashing function, maps from the key space into the bucket address space. We want h(K) to give a uniform random distribution while mapping K into the bucket addresses. After generating an address h(K) the address is used to enter the address space. This entering of the address space with h(K) is called probing. When the same h(K) is used to enter the address space more than one time, the sequence is called a probe sequence.

The address h(K), where K is the key, is called the home address. A distinct keys are mapped into the same bucket slot are called synonyms. Such an occurrence is called a collision at the home address. If a one-to-one map can be constructed then the function is said to be a direct addressing function. When the number of records in a bucket exceeds the bucket size we have an overflow. In many cases the overflow records are kept in a common area called an overflow area.

7.1. Hashing Methods

Since h(K) is random process that maps the key in the logical space into an address in the physical space many options exist for the function h(K). Remember the objective is to distribute the keys over the physical space in a

45

manner that minimizes clustering. In short, the h(K) is function defined on the binary bits. So, operations on the binary bits that represent the key directly affect the outcome for the probe address. Several bit operations are detailed for possible options in defining h(K).

7.1.1. Digit Selection

Suppose that the keys of the set of data that we are dealing with are strings of digits such as Social Security numbers that consist of nine-digits.

$$K = d_1d_2d_3d_4d_5d_6d_7d_8d_9$$

If the population that makes up the data is randomly chosen, then the chosen, then the choice of the last three digits, $d_7d_8d_9$, will give a good random distribution of values. The maximum probe address is 1000. Care must be taken in deciding which digits to select. If the population with which we are dealing is students at a university, for example, the last three digits, $d_7d_8d_9$, are probably a good choice, whereas the first three digits, $d_1d_2d_3$, are probably not. State universities tend to draw their student bodies from a single state or geographical region. The first three digits of the Social Security number are based on the geographical region in which the number was originally issued.

If the key population is known in advance, it is possible to analyze the distribution of values taken by each digit of the key. The digits participating in the hash address are then easy to select. Such an analysis is called digit analysis. Instead of choosing the last three digits, we would choose the three digits of the key whose digit analyses yield the most uniform distribution. If d_4, d_7, d_9 gave the flattest distribution, the hashing function might strip out those digits from the key and put them together to form a probe address in the range 0-999:

$$h(d_1d_2d_3d_4d_5d_6d_7d_8d_9) = d_4d_7d_9.$$

7.1.2. Division

One of the most effective hashing methods is division, which works as follows:

$$h(K) = K \bmod m = b, \text{ where } 0 \leq b \leq m - 1$$

The bit pattern of the key, regardless of its data type, is treated as an integer, divided in the integer sense by m, and the remainder of the division is used as the table address. The address b is in the range from 0 to m − 1. If m is even, all factors of m maps onto the same address. We want m to be odd to avoid this bias and increase the performance of h.

7.1.3. Multiplication

A simple method that is based on multiplication is sometimes used. Suppose that the keys are five digits in length:

$K = d1d2d3d4d5$

The key is squared by

$$d_1d_2d_3d_4d_5$$
$$x\ d_1d_2d_3d_4d_5$$
$$- - - - - - - - -$$
$$r_1r_2r_3r_4r_5r_6r_7r_8r_9r_{10}$$

The result is a 10-digit product. The function is completed by doing digit selection on the product. In most cases, the middle digits are chosen, for example, $r_4r_5r_6$.

7.1.4. Folding

Suppose that we have a five-digit key as we had in the multiplication method:

$K = d_1d_2d_3d_4d_5.$

One way to form a hash function is simply to add the individual digits of the key:

$h(K) = d_1 + d_2 + d_3 + d_4 + d_5$

The result would be in the range

$0 \leq b \leq 45$

and could be used as the index in the hash table. If a larger table is needed, it may be enlarged by adding the numbers as pairs of digits:

$h(K) = 0d_1 + d_2d_3 + d_4d_5$

The result would then be between 000 and 207. Folding is a name given to a class of methods that involves combining portions of the key to form a smaller key.

7.1.5. Character-Valued Keys

All the examples in our discussion of hashing functions assumed that the keys were some form of integer. At times, the keys are character, strings, or character-valued keys. Remember all data stored in a computer memory are simply strings of bits. For example, the ASCII code for the character 'y' is

$$1111001_2$$

which can also be interpreted as the integer value 121. The character 'y' may be typed cased in the Java Programming Language to an integer:

char tk[ ] = new char [2];   tk [0] = 'y';   int IK = (int)tk[0];

The integer IK is used in the hash function to determine the probe address for 'y'.

7.2. Collision Resolution Methods

A collision-resolution strategy, or rehashing, determines what happens when two or more objects have a collision, or hash to the same address. Algorithms detailed in this section define several collision-resolution strategies.

7.2.1. Open Addressing

An alternative solution for resolving collisions is to dispense with links entirely and instead look at other entries in the same table until the object is found or an open position is encountered, in which case one may assume that the specified key is not present in the table. This method is called open addressing. Algorithm C loads a hash table using open addressing. Algorithm S searches a hash table using open addressing.

Open Hash Load With Forward Cyclic Scan (Linear Probing)

Algorithm C. Open Hashing With Forward Cyclic Scan

A key K is hashed and stored in a table T with the hashing function h(X) = X MOD N, where X is the key and N is the maximum number of rows in T.
C1. [Initialize] for (j = 0; j <= N; ++j) T[j]=-1;
C2. [Hash the key.] i = h(K);
C3. [Probe the hash table T at i.] if (T[i] == -1) { T[i] = K; terminate;}
C4. [Look for an empty slot for the key in T.]
    if (i!= N) for (j = i+1; j<= N; ++j) if(T[j] == -1){ T[j] = K; terminate;}

C5. [Look in the lower part of T for an empty slot.]
   if (i!= 0) for (j = 0; j <= i - 1; ++j) { if (T[j] == -1) { T[j] = K; terminate;}
C6. [The hash table is full.] print ("The hash table is full."); terminate;

Open Hash Search With Forward Cyclic Scan (Linear Probing)

Algorithm S. Open Hashing Search With Forward Cyclic Scan

A key K is hashed and search T with the hashing function h(X) = X MOD N, where X is the key and N is the maximum number of rows in T.
S2. [Hash the key.] i = h(K);
S3. [Probe the table T at i.] if (T[i] == K) { print ("Found in T"); terminate;}
S4. [A hit has occurred. Look at the upper part of the table.] if (i!= N) {
   for (j = i+1; j <= N; ++j) { if (T[j] == K) print ("Found in T"); terminate;}}
S5. [Look in the lower part of T for the search key.]
   if (i!= 0) for (j = 0; j <= i - 1; ++j) { if (T[j] == K){ print ("Found in T");
   terminate;}
S6. [The search key is not in the hash table.] print ("The Search is not in the
   hash table"); terminate;

7.2.2. Chaining With Separate Lists

When a collision occurs a second probe is necessary, one based on an index obtained in a deterministic manner from the given key. There are several methods of generating secondary indices to implement collision strategies. One method is linking all entries with identical primary index h(K) together as a linked list. We call this method collision resolution by chaining with separate lists or direct chaining. Chaining with separate lists is detailed in Figure 21.

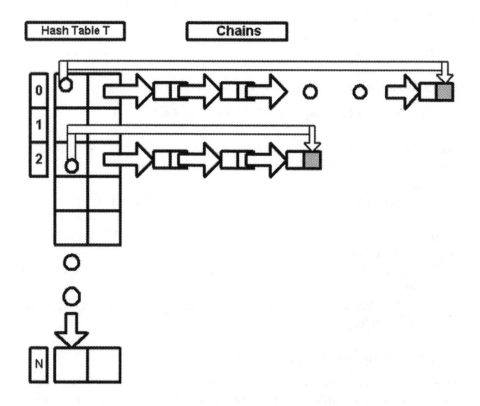

Figure 21. Chaining With Separate Lists

Load Hash Table With Chaining

Algorithm G. Hashing Load With Chaining

The table T of size N is used to store the links to the list that contain the keys that mapped onto the same cell of T. K is the new input key. The hashing function or method is h(X) = X MOD N, where X is the input key. h(X) returns the physical index used to probe the table T.

G1. [Initialize.] for (j = 0; j< N; ++j) {T[j][0] = null; T[j][1] = null;}
G2. [Hash the key.] i = h(K)
G3. [Probe the table.] if (T[i][0] == null)
    { // Get a node to start a new list.
     ListNode IG = new ListNode (null);
G4. [Store the object key in the node.] infoi(IG, K, 0);
G5. [Connect the node to the hash table.] T[i][1] = IG;

G6. [Point to the end of the list.] T[i][0] = IG; terminate;
}
G7. [A collision has occurred. Store the information on the list.
Get the pointer to the end of the listlist.]IP = T[i][0];
G8. [Get a node] ListNode IG = Listnode (null);
G9. [Insert the object in Data0] infoi(IG, K, 0);
G10. [Connect the node to the current list.] CONS (IP, IG);
G11. [Store the pointer to the end of the list.] T[I][0]= IG; terminate;

Hash Retrieval With Chaining

Algorithm S. Hashing Retrieve With Chaining

The table T of size N is used to store the links to the list that contain the keys or objects that mapped onto the same cell of T. Nodes for the list are used K is the search key. The hashing function or method is $h(X) = X$ MOD N, where X is the input key. $h(X)$ returns the physical index used to probe the table T.
S2. [Hash the key.] $i = h(K)$.
S2. [Probe the table.]
if (T[i][0] == 0)
{ print ("The key is not in the hash table."); terminate;}
S3. [Look for the key in the list. Get the pointer to the list, walk on the list,
and check the object for the key.] IP = T[i][1];
S4. [Compare the objects in the list to the search object.]
while (IP!= null)
{ G = info (IP, 0); if(G == K) {print ("Found"); Terminate;}
S5. [Move to the next node on the list.] IP = CDR(IP);} // end while
S6. [The search key is not in the hash table.] print ("Not Found"); Terminate;

7.2.3. Quadratic Probing

The whole idea of hashing is to map the keys on the physical space to minimize clustering or collisions. One way to minimize clustering is to use a quadratic function on a sequence of indices for probing. Define $b_0 = h(K)$; $b_i = (b_0 + i^2)$ mod N, where $i > 0$. This is called quadratic probing and it avoids primary clustering. A disadvantage is that in probing not all table entries are searched, that is, upon insertion a free slot may not be found although there are some left. Quadratic probing visits at least half of the table if its size N is a prime number.

7.3. Summary

The load factor is $\alpha = N/M$, where N is the number of records currently in the table. Number of accesses verses the load factor is detailed in Figure 22.

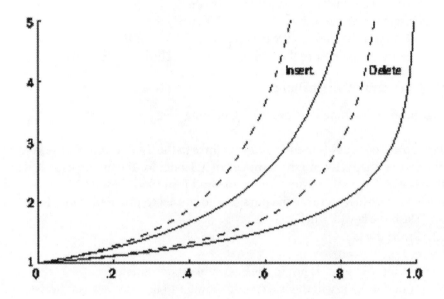

Figure 22. Number of Accesses Verses Load Factor

Hashing analysis theoretical results are detailed in Figure 23.

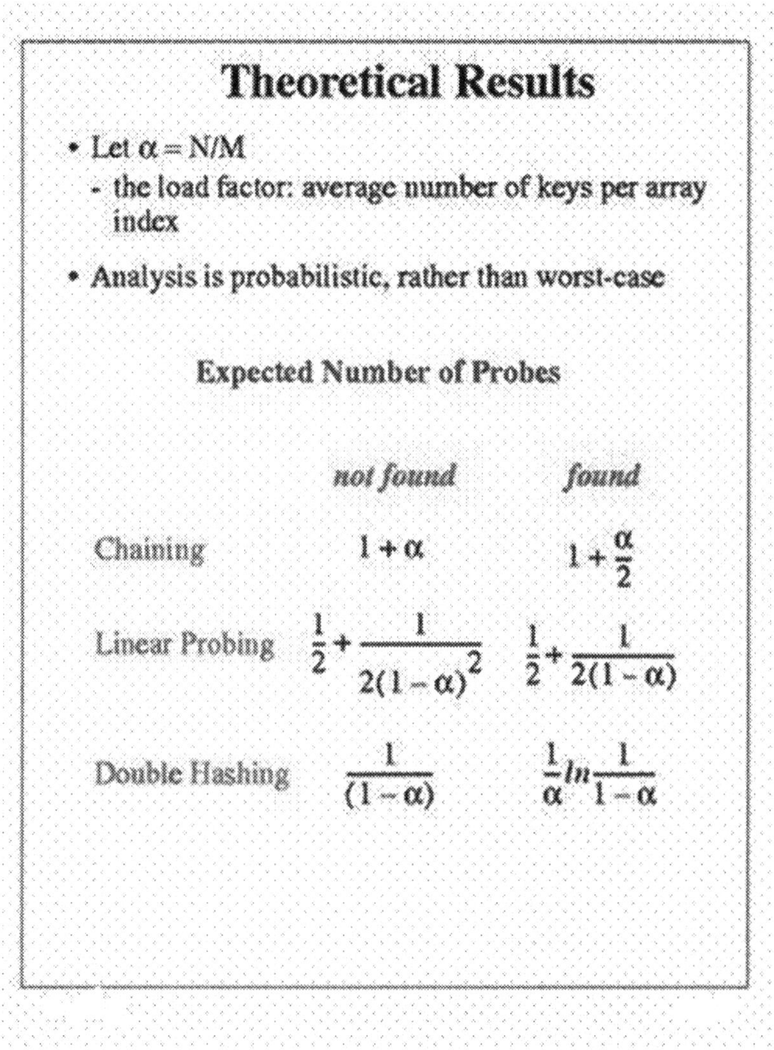

Theoretical Results

- Let $\alpha = N/M$
  - the load factor: average number of keys per array index

- Analysis is probabilistic, rather than worst-case

Expected Number of Probes

	not found	*found*
Chaining	$1 + \alpha$	$1 + \dfrac{\alpha}{2}$
Linear Probing	$\dfrac{1}{2} + \dfrac{1}{2(1-\alpha)^2}$	$\dfrac{1}{2} + \dfrac{1}{2(1-\alpha)}$
Double Hashing	$\dfrac{1}{(1-\alpha)}$	$\dfrac{1}{\alpha} ln \dfrac{1}{1-\alpha}$

Figure 23. Hashing Performance Analysis

The expected number of probes verses the load factor is detailed in Figure 24.

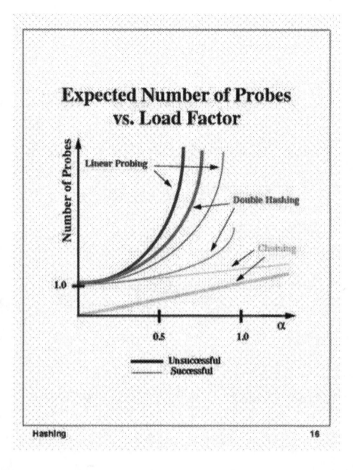

Figure 24. Expected Number of Probes Verses Load Factor

7.4. Exercises

1. Use the DSM to implement an algorithm as a method or load a hash table with double linked chaining for collision management. Load the information from a hard disk file called HAS.DAT into the table H. The data stored as one number per record in HAS.DAT are 32, 18, 20, 10, 226, 172, 50, 456, 691, 30, 100, 80, 340, 234, 349, 986, 234, 198, 275, 384. HAS.DAT has 20 data items; however, the input must be designed for an unknown number of items.

2. Use the DSM to implement an algorithm as methods to search for keys from the hard disk file KEY.DAT in table H. The data stored as one number per record in KEY.DAT are 2, 691, 234, 1000, 10. KEY.DAT has 3 data items; however, the input must be designed for an unknown number of items. Post all the output in one GUI dialog box as sentences with one key per line.

3. Use the DSM to implement methods to collect the necessary statistics to calculate the load factor, the average number of probes needed to find a value that is in the table, and the average number of probes needed to fine a value that is not in the table. Integrate these methods in problems one and two.

8

Text Processing

8.1. Pattern Matching Algorithms

Consider a text string T of length and a pattern string P of length m. Find whether P is a substring of T. We desire to search T on a character by character basis. The outcome of the algorithm is that the pattern P does not exist in T or it returns an integer indicating the starting index in T of the substring matching P. The elements of T and P belong to a universal alphabet called Σ. The Σ is finite with $|\Sigma|$ as a fixed finite constant.

Pattern matching algorithms are classified by their character comparison and shifts that define the next step in the matching process.

Brute Force

This algorithm tests all possible placements of P relative to T until a match is found.

Algorithm F. Brute-Force Pattern Matching

T is the input target string of length n. P is the input pattern string of length m. The output is the starting index i of the first substring of T matching P, or an indicator that P is not a substring of T.
F1. [For each candidate index in T] for (I = 0; I <= n – m; ++i)
{
F2. [Initialize the pattern search] j = 0;
F3. [Search for P in T] while (j < m and T[I + j] == P[j])
{

F4. [Increment the pattern index] j = j + 1;
F5. [Is the pattern P a substring of T?] if (j == m) return i;
   } //end while
   } //end for
F6. [P is not a substring of T] return "P is not a substring of T";

Performance

The outer for-loop of algorithm F is executed at most n – m + 1 times. The inner while-loop is executed at most m times. The running time of the brute-force method is)((n – m + 1)m), which is O(nm). The worst case occurs when the pattern P exist at the nth character of T or when n and m are approximately equal.

A text string: TWO ROADS DIVERGED IN A YELLOW WOOOD ROADS

A pattern string: ROADS

An example of the Brute Force algorithm is detailed in Figure 25.

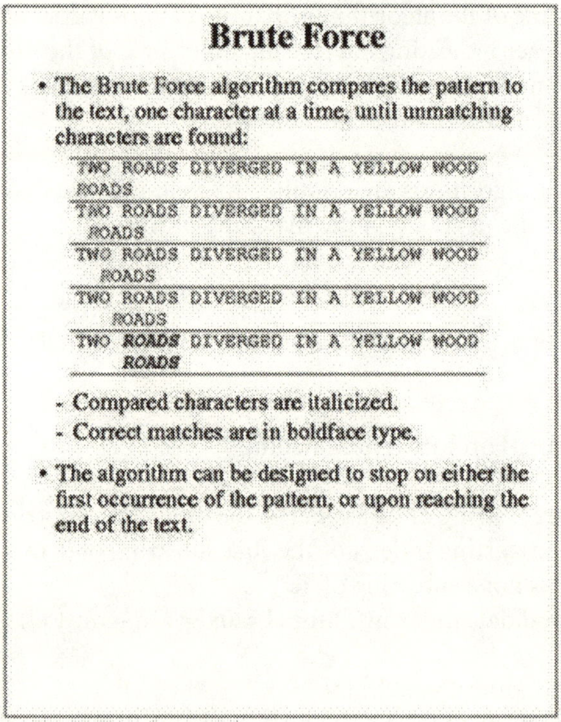

Figure 25. Brute Force Example

The Boyer-Moore Algorithm

The Boyer-Moore (BM) algorithm is designed to improve the running time of the Brute-Force algorithm. This is accomplished by adding two potentially time-saving heuristics. The heuristics are:

Looking-Glass Heuristic: When testing a possible placement of P against T, begin the comparisons from the end of P and move backward to the front of P.

Character-Jump Heuristic: During the testing of a possible placement of P against T, a mismatch of text character $T[i] = c$ with the corresponding pattern character $P[j]$ is handled as follows. If c is not contained anywhere in P, then shift P completely past $T[i]$ for it cannot match any character in P. Otherwise, shift P until an occurrence of character c in P gets aligned with $T[i]$.

Define a function last (c) that takes a character c from the alphabet and characterizes how far we may shift the pattern P if a character equal to c is found in the text that does not match the pattern. If c is in P, last (c) is the index of the last (right most) occurrence of c in P. Otherwise, we define last (c) = -1.

Algorithm BM Boyer-Moore Algorithm

T is the input text string with n characters and P a pattern string with m characters. The output is the starting index of the first substring of T matching P, or an indication that P is not a substring of T.
BM1. [Compute function last] $i = m - 1$; $j = m - 1$;
BM2. [Check P in T] repeat BM2 to BM3
    if $(P[j] == T[i])$ then
      if $(j == 0)$ then
        return i; //a match found
      else $\{i = i - 1; j = j - 1;\}$
      else $\{i = i + m - \min(j, 1 + last (T[i]); j = m - 1;\}$ //jump step
BM3. [End of repeat] until $i > n - 1$
BM4. [No match of P in T] return "There is no substring of T matching P."

We may perform many comparisons while testing a potential placement of a pattern against the text. We discover a pattern character that does not match in the text. The information gained by these comparisons is thrown away we start over again from scratch with the next incremental placement of the pattern. The Knuth-Morris-Pratt (KMP) algorithm avoids this waste of information and achieves a running time of O(n + m), which is optimal in the worst case. In the worst case any pattern matching algorithm will have to examine all the characters of the text and all the characters of the pattern at least once. This algorithm is detailed in [8].

8.2. Practical Extraction Language

The ease and power of Practical Extraction Language (Perl)'s pattern matching is one its true strengths and a big reason why Perl is as popular as it is. Almost every script you write in Perl will have some kind of pattern matching operation because so often you want to seek something out, and then take an action when you find it. We are including Perl because it is used in many Bioinformatics and Genomics projects. Perl is introduced for it search and string capabilities. Perl is referred to as a script language. Additional information on Perl is contained in [7]. There are many script languages with similar pattern matching and search capabilities. Python is a freely available, very high-level, interpreted script language developed by Guido van Rossum. It combines a clear syntax with powerful (but optional) object-oriented semantics. Python is widely available and highly portable. Additional information on Python is detailed in [8].

Practical Extraction Language (Perl) is a general purpose computer language ideally suited to handling words and text. Perl is admired for staying simple when you need to do simple things.

Matching and substitution are very important because this is how you do editing "on the fly". This is how you create content customized for an audience. Matching and then substituting is just the way to do it.

Pattern matching, in Perl at least, is the process of looking through sections of text for particular words, letters-within-words, character sequences, numbers, strings of numbers, and working with them.

In general, whatever you are seeking can be represented as a text pattern, whether it is a very explicit one, like looking for a specific word like "goodness", or a much more general one, like looking for a North American phone number: three digits, three digits, then four digits.

These more complicated search expressions fall into the category of "regular expressions". This is an extremely important part of Perl.

8.2.1. Matching and Substitution in Perl

When you do a pattern match, you need three things:
- the text you are searching through
- the pattern you are looking for
- a way of linking the pattern with the searched text

As a simple example, let's say you want to see whether a string variable has the value of "success". Here's how you could write the problem in Perl:

```
$word = "success";

if ($word =~ m/success/) {
        print "Found success\n";
} else {
        print "Did not find success\n";
}
```

There are two things to note here.

First, the "=~" construct, called the binding operator, is what binds the string being searched with the pattern that specifies the search. The binding operator links these two together and causes the search to take place.

Next, the "m/success/" construct is the matching operator, m//, in action. The "m" stands for matching to make it easy to remember. The slash characters here are the "delimiters". They surround the specified pattern. In m/success/, the matching operator is looking for a match of the letter sequence: success.

Generally, the value of the matching statement returns 1 if there was a match, and 0 if there wasn't. In this example, the pattern matches so the returned value is 1, which is a true value for the if-statement, so the string "Found success\n" is printed.

8.2.2. Regular Expressions

In the previous example, the expression /success/ is a very simple example of a more general concept of the "regular expression".

All patterns matching in Perl is based on this concept of regular expressions. Regular expressions are an important part of computer science, and entire books are devoted to the topic. Regular expressions form a standard way of expressing almost any text pattern unambiguously.

Luckily, for our purposes regular expressions can start out simple. Once you have these key concepts mastered, you'll be able to find out and learn more about them on your own through many online resources. The power of regular expressions starts to become clear when you discover they can represent words and phrases but also far more general patterns of text.

Note In many of the following examples of pattern matching; only the pattern match is shown. If you put any of these patterns into effect you still have to use a variable and the binding operator. Usually. ;-)

Plain Character Expressions

Many letters and characters can represent themselves in a matching pattern, so often just the plain word by itself will act as a regular expression. E.g. /success/, /failure/, and /nearly all plain text/ are all pattern matches that are very straightforward in their meaning.

It's important to note that without any additional qualification, these search patterns can occur **anywhere** in the string being searched, so /success/ would match any of the strings: "success", "This sentence contains success", and "unsuccessful". Many times, plain vanilla search patterns like this are adequate for the job. Virtually any plain English word without any punctuation can be used as a regular expression to represent itself as a search pattern.

Special Characters

Some special characters or combinations of characters have a special meaning and do not represent themselves. This is what gives regular expressions their power. For example, the lowly period does not stand for a period in a match. Instead, it stands for **any** character.

The pattern /b.g/ would match "bag", "big", "bug", etc, as well as **any** other sequence: "b2g", "b&g", "b]g" and so on. It would match "b.g" itself, where . does represent a period. /b.g/ would also match longer expressions: "bigger", "bug swatter".

Matching simply means "found somewhere, anywhere, within the searched string". You can use special characters to specify the position where the search pattern must be located.

A ^ character stands for the beginning of the searched string, so:
/^success/ would match "success" but not "unsuccessful".
A $ character stands for the end of the searched string, so:
/success$/ would match "unsuccessful" but not "successful".
Using both ^ and $ together nails the pattern down at both ends, so:
/^success$/ will only match the exact string "success".
Other special characters include:
\ - a form of a "quote" character
| - alternation, used for "or'ing"
() - grouping matched elements
[] - character class

The first character, "\", is used in combination with special letters to take away their special meaning. E.g.:

\. will match a period
\$ will match a dollar sign
\^ will match a caret
\\ will match a backslash

and so on.

The pipe symbol "|" is used to provide alternatives:
/good|bad/ will match either "good vibes" or "bad karma".
The parentheses group matched elements, so
/(good|bad) example/
is the same as searching simultaneously for
/good example/ or
/bad example/
Without the ()'s, this would be the same as searching simultaneously for
/good/ or
/bad example/
The square brackets indicate a class of characters, so
/^[abcdefg]/ would match any strings beginning with the letters a through g. This can also be written in shorthand as /^[a-g]/.

Special Backslash Combination Characters:

The backslash character is not just used to "quote metacharacters" (in other words to remove their special meaning) as above. It is also used in conjunction with non-special characters to give them a special meaning. For instance

\t is a tab character
\n is a newline character
\d is any digit
\D is any non-digit
\s is a whitespace character
\S is any nonwhitespace character

You'll find yourself using these backslash combinations a lot in practice.

Repetition Characters

The expressions above show you how to match certain characters, but they don't allow you to control how many matches should be made at once. Matching repetition is controlled by a few other special characters:

+ means 1 or more matches
* means 0 or more matches
? means 0 or 1 matches
{n} exactly n matches
{m,n} m to n matches

The best way to learn Regular Expressions is by example, so let's go on to see how these amazing things can be put to work together in the next section.

Examples of Regular Expressions

To try out what we learned in Regular Expressions it would be good to see a few pattern matches in practice to see how they go together. Regular expressions and meanings are detailed in Figure 26.

Regular Expression	Meaning
/a.c/	the letter a followed by any character then c
/a+c/	one or more a's followed by c
/a*c/	zero or more a's followed by c, so even "c" matches.

/a?c/	zero or one a followed by c: "ac" or "c"
/a.+c/	a followed by one or more characters, then c
/a.*c/	a followed by zero or more characters, then c, so even "ac" matches.
/a|bc/	"a" or "bc"
/(a|b)c/	"ac" or "bc"
/(a|b)+c/	one or more a's or b's, followed by c: ac, bc, aac, abc, aaac, abbabababbac.
/(a|A)\ssample\smatch/	"A" or "a" followed by one whitespace character, then "sample", then one whitespace character, then "match".
/\d\d\d-\d\d\d-\d\d\d\d/	Any phone number like this: 250-123-1234
/\(\d\d\d\)\s\d\d\d\-\d\d\d\d/	Any North American phone number like this: (250) 123-1234
/\(\d{3}\)\s\d{3}-\d{4}/	As above, but using the count specifier
/<title.*title>/	An html title tag, with any title. The .* match would include the > and <\ characters
/<title>.*<\/title>/	An html title tag, with any title. The </title> tag needs a backslash quote in front of the slash, \/, to prevent the slash from being taken as the end of the pattern The .* match would include only the title text, not the > and </ as above
/first.*second.*third/	Any sequence of text with the word first before the word second before the word third. Any or no characters can lie in between the words
/^\t+\S+\s*/	Any line of text starting with one or more tabs, containing at least one nonwhitespace characer, followed by no or some whitespace
/^b[aeiouy]+t/	Any line of text starting with b followed by any combination of 1 or more vowels and then the letter t/

Figure 26. Regular Expressions and Meanings

If you are comfortable with the examples in Figure 26, continue on to learn how to perform substitutions.

8.2.3. Substituting New Text For Old

Perl's can substitute text just as easily as it can match it, but instead of using the plain matching operator m//, you use the substitution operator, s///.

When a match is made, Perl knows which characters matched, and it sets up built-in variables to point at the starting position and the ending position of the match in the searched string. For example, if you had:

    $text = "Here is some text"

and you did a match on the regular expression /some.*/, like this:

    $text =~ m/some.*/

then Perl would know that the matched string was "some text", and it would know that the match started at the 9th character and ended at the 17th.

When you use the substitution operator, s///, Perl uses that positional information to know which characters to replace with the substitution text.

Simple substitution

The substitution operator has two specifications: on the left, the matching regular expression like the matching operator, and on the right, the substitution value.

Let's say you wanted to change the first occurrence of the word dog into cat in the string variable $story. This is simple:

    $story =~ s/dog/cat/;

Your substituted string does not have to be the same length as the matched string. You could put in more letters or fewer:

    s/a short phrase/a much longer phrase/
    s/1999/MCMXCIX/
    s/Twenty first century/21st century/

You can also look for a more abstract pattern and replace it. Let's say you wanted to edit any 3 digits and replace them with dummy values, of nnn. You could use a substitution operator like this:

s/\d\d\d/nnn/;

This would take any sequence of 3 digits and replace replace them with the letters "nnn".

Let's say you wanted to edit all phone numbers and replace them with dummy values. You could use a substitution operator like this:

s/\d{3}-\d{3}-\d{4}/123-123-1234/;

This would take any sequence of 3 digits, minus sign, 3 digits, minus sign, and 4 digits and replace that phone number with 123-123-1234.

For any of the matching expressions in the table on the previous page of examples, we could just as easily have specified some text to replace it with, by using the s/// operator instead of just the m// operator.

Deletion

You can use s/// for deleting things too. Just use an empty value for the substitution. Here's how you might delete an html comment consisting of everything between <!-- and -->:

s/<!--.*-->//;

Isn't that amazingly simple?!

Remembering Matched Values

Suppose you wanted to match on something and modify it, but re-use part of what you matched on. Let's say you wanted to replace an occurrence of boys with boyz or girls with girlz. You could do this in separate passes like this:

s/boys/boyz/;
s/girls/girlz/;

or alternatively, since TIMTOWTDI, you could match on either boy or girl, and remember what it was you matched on, like this:

s/(boy|girl)s/$1z/;

The $1 is called a positional parameter, and it is an internal variable maintained automatically by Perl to represent whatever was matched within the brackets of the search expression. Here, we are looking for either boy or girl followed by an s. We want to replace it by whatever we find, with a z substituted for the s. The $1 parameter will remember whichever word matches and will put it in the substitution.

You can remember more than one matching expression. In fact you can remember up to 9 expressions in the variables the $1 through $9. I have never had occasion to go past $4, so 9 variables is probably more than enough.

As an example of remembering two matches consider this method of getting rid of potential visitors:

s/(dog|cat)s are (invited|welcome)/$1s are not $2/;

Note that $1 represents either dog or cat, whichever was found, and $2 represents either invited or welcome, whichever was found. Note also that Perl is smart enough to know that the string "$1s" means the $1 variable followed by an "s". It does not get confused into thinking you meant a variable with the name of $1s.

8.2.4. Basic Perl Regular Expressions Examples

Match a word: \w+

```
if ('One word' =~ /\w+/) {
        print "Matched $&\n";
}
#Matched One
```

Match an integer: [-+]?\d+

```
$_ = 'One value: +23.45';
if (/[-+]?\d+/) {
        print "Matched $&\n";
}
#"Matched +23"
```

Match a number that has 3 to 5 digits: \d{3,5}

```
if (12345 =~ /^\d{3,5}$/) {
        print "Number within range\n";
}
```

Match everything between foo and bar: greedy version

```
$_ = 'brave fools embark on travel through bare
desert';
print $& if /foo.*bar/;
#prints "fools embark on travel through bar"
```

Match everything between foo and bar: non greedy version

```
$_ = 'brave fools embark on travel through bare
desert';
print $& if /foo.*?bar/;
#prints "fools embar"
```

Here is the complete specification for a perl regex match operation:

```
m/expr/gsimox;
```

You can choose to leave out the *m* (which stands for *match*, by the way) and just use /pattern/ which is what you normally do. However, perl allows you to use ANY character as the pattern delimiter, and allows you to write the regex in a more readable manner. Here are some regexes, all of which match the same pattern: finding the directory name of a file.

```
1.  /(\/[^\s]+)\/[^\/\s]+/;
2.  m,(/[^\s]+)/[^/\s]+,;
3.  m{
        (/[^\s]+)        #a slash followed by
any non space character
        /                #start of filename
part
        [^/\s]+          #a filename (assume no
spaces in the filename)
    }x;
```

As we see from regex 1, match patterns can be very hairy. The reason why we had all those leaning toothpicks(\/) was due to the fact that the pattern was delimited by a /. In such cases, if you want to match a literal forward slash, you need to quote/escape it with the \ character. Regex 2 is clearer because it now uses comma characters to delimit the pattern. This, you don't have to quote the /. Even after this substantial improvement in readability, the pattern looks difficult. Regex 3 is probably the easiest for *humans* to parse. We don't offer any explanation, as it is self-evident. See below for more details on the /x modifier. With such powerful constructs perl allows you to match almost any type of pattern (*nested* patterns are one exception).

However, a match is not the only reason to use a regex. Once you perform a match, you can actually substitute whatever you matched, with anything else you may want to change it to. Here is the spec for the regex **Substitution** operator:

```
s{expr}{replacement}egsimox;
```

8.3. Exercises

1. Use the DSM to implement a program as a method or set of methods to locate a pattern in a text string using a Brute Force algorithm. The text string is AAAAAAAAAAAAAAAAAAAAAAAAAAAAH. The pattern string is AAAAH. Display the results in a GUI dialog box.

2. This is a no cost problem for your personal computer running the Windows, UNIX, or Linux and other operating systems. Download the Practical Extraction Language (Perl) translator with documentation from http://www.ActiveState.com. Install Perl and configure your machine. Download the Perl examples from http://www.cookwood.com. Execute and review the source code for several string examples. Use these examples as a tutorial for Perl.

9

File Access Methods

Most operating systems provide a set of basic file organizations that are popular with the users of the system. The three most common types of organizations are sequential, indexed sequential, and direct. The presentation of each of these organizations begins with a description of its file structure.

9.1. Sequential Organizations

A disk cylinder surface index is maintained for the primary key. Indexed Sequential Access Method (ISAM) is the name associated with this access method. In order to efficiently retrieve records based on other keys, it is necessary to maintain additional indexes on the remaining keys (i.e., secondary keys). The structure of these indexes may correspond to any of the alternative index techniques. The ISAM is detailed in Figure 27.

Indexed Sequential File

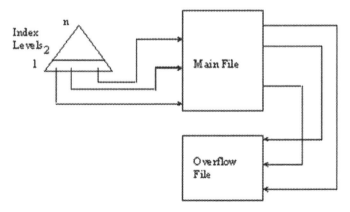

Figure 27. Indexed Sequential File Organization

Indexed File

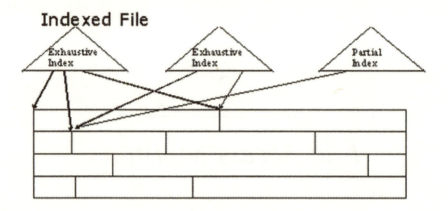

Figure 28. Indexed File Organization

In a sequential file, records are stored one after the other on a storage device. Of course, a sequential type of storage representation is not new to us. Some options are the sequential representation of characters in a string, of arrays, and of certain linear and nonlinear lists. Because sequential allocation is conceptually simple, yet flexible enough to cope with many of the problems associated with handling large volumes of data, a sequential file has been the most popular basic file structure used in the data-processing industry. Most types of external storage devices support a sequential-file organization. Some devices, by their physical nature, can only support sequential files. Information is stored on a magnetic tape as a continuous series of records along the length of the tape. Accessing a particular record requires the accessing of all previous records in the file. Other devices which are strictly sequential in nature are paper tape readers, card readers, tape cassettes, and line printers.

Magnetic disks and drums provide both direct and sequential access to records, and hence support sequential files along with other types of files. A sequential file is physically placed on a drum or disk by storing the sequence of records in adjacent locations on a track. Of course, if the file is larger than the amount of space available on a track, then the records are stored on adjacent tracks. This notion of physical adjacency can be extended to cylinders and even to complete storage devices where more than one device is attached to a common control unit. A sequential file organization is detailed in Figure 29.

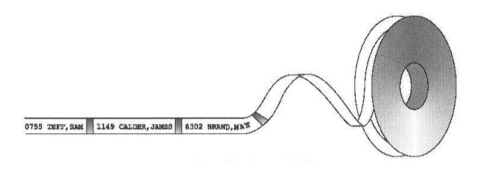

Figure 29. Sequential File Organization

9.2. Random Organizations

Records are stored at random locations on disks. This randomization could be achieved by any one of several techniques. Some of these techniques are direct addressing, directory lookup and hashing.

9.2.1. Direct Addressing

In direct addressing with equal size records, the available disk space is divided out into nodes large enough to hold a record. The numeric value of the primary key is used to determine the node into which a particular record is to be stored. No index on this key is needed. With primary key = Employee #, the record for Employee # = 259 will be stored in node 259. With this organization, searching and deleting a record given its primary key value requires only one disk access. Updating a record requires two: one to read and another to write back the modified record. When variable size records are being used an index can be set up with pointers to actual records on disk. The number of accesses needed using this scheme is one more than for the case when memory was divided into fixed size nodes. The storage management scheme becomes more complex. The space efficiency of direct accessing depends on the identifier density n/T, where n = number of distinct primary key values in the file, and T = total number of possible primary key values. In the case of internal tables, this density is usually very low and direct addressing was very space inefficient. Figure 30 and Figure 31 detail performance on random access methods. These graphics and other information are detailed by Olson [6].

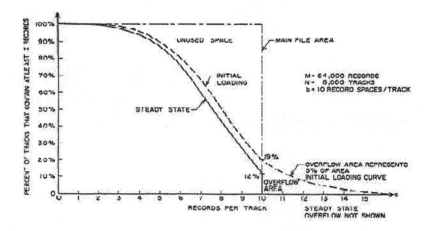

Figure 30. Percentage of Tracks Having Various Number of Records

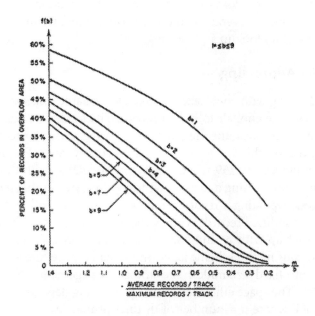

Figure 31. The Percentage of Records in Overflow Area as a Function of the Average and the Maximum Number of Records per Track.

9.2.2. Directory Look Up

This is very similar to the scheme of direct addressing with variable size records. Now, however, the index is not of direct access type but is a dense index maintained using a structure suitable for index operations. Retrieving data involves searching the index for the record address and then accessing the record itself. The storage management scheme will depend on whether fixed size or variable size nodes are being used. Except when the identifier density is almost 1, this scheme makes a more efficient utilization of space than does direst addressing. However it requires more accesses for retrieval and update, since index searching will generally require more than one access. In both direct addressing and directory lookup, some provision must be made for collisions when two or more records have the same primary key value. In many applications the possibility of collisions is ruled out since the primary key value uniquely identifies a record. Directory look up is detailed in Figure 32, as a special case of hashing. In this case, hashing is applied to the directory to store and locate file names.

9.2.3. Hashing Organization

Hashing Organization uses the same techniques used for a hash index. Divide the available space to handle overflows. The available file space is divided into buckets and slots. Some space may have to be set aside for an overflow area in case chaining is being used to handle overflows. When variable size records are present, the number of slots per bucket will be only a rough indicator of the number of records a bucket can hold. The actual number will vary dynamically with the size of records in a particular bucket.

Random organization on the primary key overcomes the difficulties of sequential organizations. Insertions and deletions become relatively trivial operations. At the same time, random organizations lose the advantages of a sequential ordered organization. Batch processing of queries becomes inefficient as the records are not maintained in order of the primary key. The hashing file organization is detailed in Figure 32.

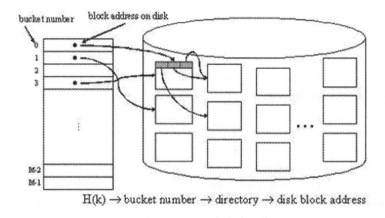

H(k) → bucket number → directory → disk block address

Figure 32. Hash File Organization

9.3. Linked Organization

Differs from sequential organization essentially in that the logical sequence of records is generally different from the physical sequence. In a Sequential Organization the i-th record of the file is at location Li then the (i+ 1)-th record is in the next physical location Li + c, where c may be the length of the i-th record or some constant that determines the inter record spacing. In a linked organization the next logical record is obtained by following a link value from the present record. Linking records together in order of increasing primary key value facilitates easy insertion and deletion. Searching for a record with a given primary key value is difficult when no index is available, since the only search possible is a sequential search. To facilitate searching on the primary key as well as on secondary keys it is customary to maintain several indexes, one for each key. Linked file organization is detailed in Figure 33.

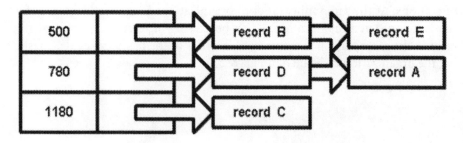

Figure 33. Linked File Organization

10

Inverted File

In many cases, it is desired to organize the records of a database to reflect database characteristics and database usage. The importance of these organizations becomes clear when one key is associated with more than one record and many keys are associated with the same record. Under these conditions, it is necessary to store the records in a structure that maximizes the use of the storage space occupied by the records on the direct access device and minimizes the time required to process the records.

Lowe [4] studied the influence of data base characteristics and usage on direct access file organization. In this study, he derived measures of performance for an inverted file which is a file organization derived from the chained organization by decreasing the length of each chain to one and correspondingly increasing the directory size to include for each key word as many entries as there are records characterized by that key word. The analysis used a function to characterize the database and a function to characterize the use of the database. All measures are developed using these functions and combinations of the assumption of uniform distribution and a qualitative rank- probability relationship called Zipf's Law [5].

The load time, retrieval time, update time, and memory utilization are investigated for direct access inverted files. An inverted file is detailed in Figure 34.

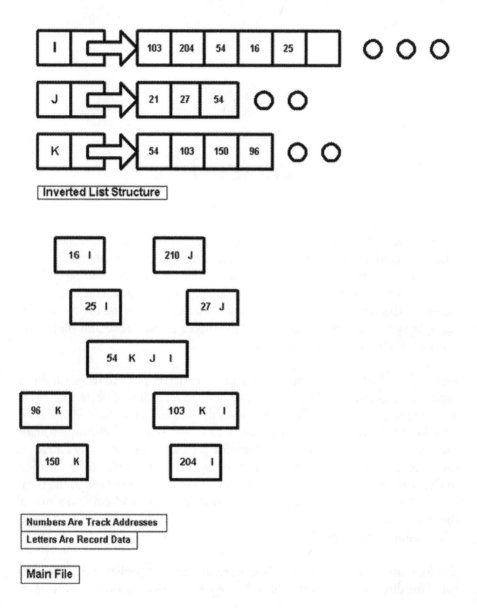

Figure 34. Inverted File Structure

10.1. Load an Inverted File

In this section the inverted file is loaded from a main file F. The load algorithm for an inverted file must include those factors that are related to the basic use of the file. The basic factors related to the use of inverted files are file loading, retrieving items from the file, file update, and storage space requirements. File update consists of file operations involving inserting and deleting items.

The time required to load an inverted file is called load time. This process involves actually inverting the file if an inverted copy is not available. For large files the inverting operation requires a large amount of computer time.

From time to time information is deleted and inserted into the file. The time spent deleting and inserting information is called the update time. In this process records are changed one-by-one on demand. Generally, updating the inverted file is an expensive operation.

Storage space is a critical factor that must be considered when using an inverted file. This is critical because the original file and the inverted file must be kept on the direct access storage device.

Algorithm I quantifies the work done while inverting a file with the file and the inverted file stored on a direct access storage device. Records are read one item at-a-time and the item and track address are passed to Algorithm I to update the inverted lists. At the end of the process that invoked Algorithm I the Table T and the B are written to the direct access device. The track address of the location of T and B is stored in the link variable V.

A frequency function $g(j)$ is used to collect a count of the occurrence of items in the file. The file is inverted on every item in the file to allow retrieval of any item. When the algorithm terminates, the inverted file and its structure are on the direct access storage device pointed to by V.

The node structure of the inverted structure is detailed in Figure 35. The inverted list is detailed in Figure 34.

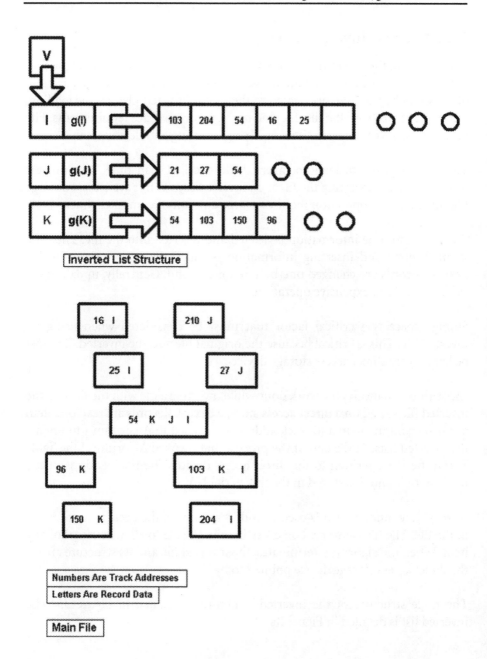

Figure 35. Inverted File

Algorithm I. Load Inverted File

The table T of size N is used to store the links to the buffers that contain the track addresses of the keys that mapped onto the same cell of T. K is the new input key and E is the track address that contains K. The hashing function or method is h(X) = X MOD N, where X is the input key. h(X) returns the physical index used to probe the table T. Initially T is setup with: for (j = 0; j< N; ++j) {T[j][0] = null; T[j][1] = null; }.

I1. [Hash the key.] i = h(K)
I2. [Probe the table.] if (T[i][0] == null)
    { // Get a node to start a new list.
    ListNode IG = new ListNode (null);
I4. [Store the object key in the node Data0.] infoi(IG, K, 0);
I6. [Update g(K) in Data1.] Object GA = info(IG, 1); GA = GA + (Object)1;
    infoi(IG, GA, 1);
I5. [Store the Track Address in the Associated Buffer] B[i][g[K] = E;
I6. [Connect the Node to T.] T[i][0] = IG; terminate;
    }
    if (i!= N) for (j = i + 1; j <= N; ++j)
    {
I7. [A collision has occurred. Get the Store Key.] IG = T[i][0]; GA = info(IG, 0);
    if (GA == K)
        {
I8. [Update g(K) in Data1.] Object GA = info(IG, 1); GA = GA + (Object)1;
        infoi(IG, GA, 1);
I9. [Store the Track Address in the Associated Buffer] B[i][g[K] = E;
        terminate;
        }
    if (i!= 0) for (j = 0; j <= i - 1; ++j)
    {
I10. [A collision has occurred. Get the Store Key.] IG = T[i][0]; GA = info(IG, 0);
    if (GA == K)
        {
I11. [Update g(K) in Data1.] Object GA = info(IG, 1); GA = GA + (Object)1;
        infoi(IG, GA, 1);
I12. [Store the Track Address in the Associated Buffer] B[i][g[K] = E;
        terminate;
        }
I13. [Table is full Message.] print ("The table is full."); terminate

10.2. Search an Inverted File

Algorithm U. Search an Inverted File

The links to the key buffers are stored in T of size N. The number of track addresses for a key K is stored in T. The buffers contain the track addresses of the keys that mapped onto the same cell of T. K is the search key. On return R contains the track addresses for key K and M contains the number of track addresses for the key K. The hashing function or method is $h(X) = X$ MOD N, where X is the input key. $h(X)$ returns the physical index used to probe the table T.

U1. [Hash the key.] i = h(K)

U2. [Probe the table.] if (T[i][0] == null)
   {

U4. [The key K is not in the inverted file.] print ("The key is not in the inverted file"); terminate;
   }
   if (i != N) for (j = i + 1; j <= N; ++j)
   {

U7. [A collision has occurred. Get the Store Key.] IG = T[i][0]; GA = info(IG, 0);
     if (GA == K)
      {

U8. [Get g(K) from Data1.] Object GA = info(IG, 1);

U9. [Transfer the track addresses to R.] for (c = 0; c <= GA; ++c) R[c] = B[i][c];
     terminate;
      }
   if (i != 0) for (j = 0; j <= i - 1; ++j)
   {

U10. [A collision has occurred. Get the Store Key.] IG = T[i][0]; GA = info(IG, 0);
     if (GA == K)
      {

U11. [Get g(K) from Data1.] Object GA = info(IG, 1);

U12. [Transfer the track addresses to R.] for (c = 0; c <= GA; ++c) R[c] = B[i][c];
     terminate;
      }

U13. [Table is full Message.] print ("The key is not in the inverted file."); terminate

The search of the inverted file for a key K was conducted without reading the main file. The number of occurrences of the key K in the file was obtained without reading the main file. Conjunction queries of any keys yield the number of occurrences in the inverted file without reading the main file. Disjunction queries of any keys yield the number of occurrences without reading the main file.

10.3. Storage Requirements

Let the total number of distinct items used to characterize the entire data base be σ. Number the distinct item names in such a way that every item name is identified by a unique number $1 \leq j \leq \sigma$, and the rank of the jth item name is j.

If g(j) is the total number of times that the item name numbered j is used in characterizing all the items in the file, then g(j) Items are characterized by the jth item name.

A record of the inverted file may extend over more than one bucket, in which case, more than one bucket is needed to store the record. The process of placing more than one short record in one bucket is called packing. When records are packed the portion of the bucket unused is wasted.

Define n as the number of units of direct access storage required to store one item. The minimum memory requirement is

$$n \sum_{j=1}^{\sigma} g(j)$$

Let S_S be the total memory required for storage of the inverted files, including wasted memory. A bucket capacity of b yields

$$S_S(n,b) = nb \left\{ \left\lceil \sum_{j=1}^{\sigma} g(j)/b \right\rceil \right\} + \eta F,$$

where $\lceil g(j)/b \rceil$ is the smallest integer greater than or equal to g(j)/b and $N = \eta F$.

10.4. Summary

The inverted file has been generated essentially by using the chain organization with the length of each chain equal to one item. This increased the directory size to Include, for, each key, as many entries as there are items characterized by that key.

The search time is shortened by eliminating all pointers from the main file and performing most of the search in the directory. The directory search is linear in all derivations. However, other directory organizations may be used by defining A_g as the average search length for the organization.

Update time is consistent with our knowledge about updating inverted files. This is a tedious task because the accession list in the directory is maintained in a specific order.

10.5. Exercises

1. Use the DSM to implement an algorithm as a method or set of methods to invert a complete inverted file with double linked chaining. Load the information from a hard disk file called VER.DAT into the table H. Data to be inverted are stored in two element pairs defined as Data followed by a Track Address of the location on a direct access storage device. The data stored as one number per record in VER.DAT are 32, 600; 18, 800; 20, 600; 10, 950,; 26, 400; 172, 600; 50,45; 456, 950; 691, 800; 30, 300; 100, 52; 80, 45; 340, 400; 234, 350; 349, 300; 986, 65; 234, 32; 198, 82; 275, 65; 384, 350;. HAS.DAT has 40 data items; however, the input must be designed for an unknown number of items.

2. Use the DSM to implement an algorithm as methods to search for keys from the hard disk file KEY.DAT in table H. The data stored as one number per record in KEY.DAT are 2, 691, 234, 1000, 10. KEY.DAT has 3 data items; however, the input must be designed for an unknown number of items. Post all the output in one GUI dialog box as sentences with one key per line.

3. Use the DSM to implement an algorithm as methods to delete a key K from H. If the deletion removes all information from the double linked chain for a given table row set the node pointer to null.

Appendix A

List Abstract Data Type

```
//------------------------------------------------------
// Version 1.26: Class ListNode and class List definitions
//------------------------------------------------------
   import javax.swing.*;
   import java.io.*;
   class ListNode {
   // package access data so class List can access it directly
   Object data; Object data1, data2, data3, data4;
   ListNode next;
   ListNode prev;
   ListNode ptr;
   //-----------------------------------------------------
   // Constructor: Create a ListNode that refers to Object o.
   // Make the next or link address null
   //-----------------------------------------------------
   ListNode(Object o) { this(o, null); }


   //-----------------------------------------------------
   // Constructor: Create a ListNode that refers to Object o and
   // to the next ListNode in the List.
   // nextNode is a pointer to the next node
   //-----------------------------------------------------
   ListNode(Object o, ListNode nextNode)
   {
      data = o;       // this node refers to Object o
      next = nextNode; // set next to refer to next
      prev = null;
```

```
  ptr = null;
}


//---------------------------------------------
// Return a reference to the Object in this node
//---------------------------------------------
Object getObject(int i)
{Object tmp = data;
 switch (i)
  {case 0: tmp = data;
  case 1: tmp = data1;
  case 2: tmp = data2;
  case 3: tmp = data3;
  case 4: tmp = data4;
  }
 return tmp;
 }


//---------------------------------------
// Return the next node pointer or address
//---------------------------------------
ListNode getNext() { return next; }
}


//------------------------
// Class List definition
//------------------------
public class List
{
private String name; // String like "list" used in printing

// Constructor: Construct an empty List with s as the name
public List(String s)
{
 name = s;
}
//-----------------------------------------
// Constructor: Construct an empty List with
// "list" as the name
//-----------------------------------------
```

```
public List()
{ this("list");
}

public synchronized Object info(ListNode ptr, int i)
{// Return the info from a node pointed to by ptr
Object tmp = ptr.data;
  switch (i)
  { case 0: tmp = ptr.data;
    case 1: tmp = ptr.data1;
    case 2: tmp = ptr.data2;
    case 3: tmp = ptr.data3;
    case 4: tmp = ptr.data4;
  }
  return tmp;
}
public synchronized void infoi(ListNode ptr, Object K, int i)
{ // Insert the info K into a node pointed to by ptr

  switch (i)
  { case 0: ptr.data = K;
    case 1: ptr.data1 = K;
    case 2: ptr.data2 = K;
    case 3: ptr.data3 = K;
    case 4: ptr.data4 = K;
  }
}
public synchronized ListNode CDR(ListNode ptt)
{
  return ptt.next;
}
public synchronized ListNode LCDR(ListNode ptt)
{
  return ptt.prev;
}
public synchronized void CONS(ListNode ptt, ListNode pti)
{// Connect the new node pointed to by pti to the right link of
// a node pointed to by ptt
  ptt.next= pti;
}
```

```
public synchronized void LCONS(ListNode ptt, ListNode pti)
{// Connect the new node pointed to by pti to the left link of
 // a node pointed to by ptt
   ptt.prev= pti;
}
public synchronized void ptosi(ListNode sn, ListNode ptrr)
{ // Insert the pointer info in the node
   sn.ptr = ptrr;
}
public synchronized ListNode ptoso(ListNode sn)
{ // Return the pointer info from the node
   return sn.ptr;
}


// ------------------------------------------------------------
// Place all your methods for the implementation of the
// algorithms in this section of the code
// Note:  The code above must not be altered.
// ------------------------------------------------------------
//
// ****** Do not make any code changes above this line *******
// ***********************************************************
// Insert User Java methods and Java public static void main
// ***********************************************************
} // End List Class ADT
```

Appendix B

An Input/Output Example

```java
import javax.swing.*;
import java.io.*;
class iobuf
{
//-----------------------------------------
// Setup File Reference Handle
//-----------------------------------------
private BufferedReader Ibuf (String fileName)
throws java.io.IOException
{
  // set up the basic input stream
  FileReader fr = new FileReader(fileName);
  // buffer the input stream
  BufferedReader br = new BufferedReader(fr);
  return br;
} // End Ibuf

//-----------------------------------------
// Input a Data Item
//-----------------------------------------
public static String Inf (BufferedReader br)
throws java.io.IOException
{ String inval;

  if ((inval = br.readLine())!= null)
    {
      return inval;
```

```java
    } else return null;

} // End Inf

public static void main(String args[])
 throws java.io.IOException
 { // Delcare Variables
   String foo = "AA";
   int Total=0;
   // Define a Reference Variable to the Container
   iobuf  DL = new iobuf ();
   BufferedReader tk;
   // Set the Path and Input File Name
   String FName = "C:\\spring2004\\csc426\\INFO.DAT";

   // Setup file reference handle
   tk = DL.Ibuf(FName);

   // Read an Input Data Items One-at-a-Time
   while (foo!= null)
   { // Input Data and Return String Data Value
     foo = DL.Inf (tk);

     // Add to Total
     if (foo!= null) Total = Total + Integer.parseInt(foo);

     // Post GUI With Data
     JOptionPane.showMessageDialog(null,"Value = "+foo);
   } // End while

   // Post Total Value
   JOptionPane.showMessageDialog(null,"Total of all Information = "+Total);

   // Close the Input File
   tk.close();

   // Terminate Program
   System.exit(0);

 } // End Method main
} // iobuf
```

References

1. Lyman Ott, An Introduction to Statistical Methods and Data Analysis, Duxbury Press, 1977.
2. Edward Hill, Jr., A Comparative Study of Very Large Databases, Lecture Notes in Computer Science, Volume No. 59, Springer-Verlag, 1978.
3. D. E. Knuth, The Art of Computer Programming, Volume 3, Searching and Sorting, Addison-Wesley Publishing Company, Reading, Mass., 1973.
4. T. C. Lowe, The Influence of Data Base Characteristics and Usage on Direct Access File Organization, J. ACM, 15, 4 (Oct. 1968) pp. 535-548.
5. G. K. Zipf, Human Behavior and The Principle of Least Effort, Hafner Publishing Company, (1965).
6. Charles A. Olson, Random Access File Organization for Indirectly Addressed Records, Advanced Applications, Inc., San Francisco, California.
7. Elizabeth Castro, Perl and CGI for the World Wide Web: Visual QuickStart Guide, Second Edition, http://www.peachpit.com, 2001.
8. D. E. Knuth, J. H. Morris, Jr., and V. R. Pratt, Fast Pattern Matching in Strings, SIAM JKournal opn Computing, Volume 6, No. 1, pp. 323-350, 1977.

About the Author

Dr. Edward Hill, Jr.
Associate Professor
Computer Science Department

Dr. Edward Hill, Jr. has been in the information profession since 1964. He has held technical and managerial positions in government including: Mathematician, Computer Systems Analyst, Survey Statistician, and Supervisory Survey Statistician from 1964-1996. He has worked as an Adjunct Associate Professor of Computer Science from 1978-1996 at Howard University. He has worked as an Associate Professor of Computer Science from 1996-present at Hampton University. He has been a Computer Science Consultant since 2000. Dr. Hill is a widely recognized expert in database design, computer information science, data resource management, and data-related planning, analysis, and design methods. He has taught many undergraduate and graduate courses in information management. Dr. Hill is distinguished by his ability to communicate concepts clearly, simply, and effectively to any audience detailing his experiences in computer science and other areas.

Dr. Hill is a graduate of Southern University (B.S. degree with major in mathematics/education), Atlanta University (M.S. degree with major in mathematics), and The George Washington University at Washington, DC (D.Sc. with major in Computer Science, minors in Applied Mathematics and Operations Research)

Hampton University Email: Edward.hill@hamptonu.edu

Index

0-595-31896-7

www.ingramcontent.com/pod-product-compliance
Lightning Source LLC
Chambersburg PA
CBHW051255050326
40689CB00007B/1210